THE
JAPANESE

THE
JAPANESE

A Critical Evaluation of the Character & Culture of a People

JEAN-FRANCOIS DELASSUS

HART PUBLISHING COMPANY, INC. • NEW YORK CITY

Contents

THE
JAPANESE

The Game of Appearances

We are all familiar with the romantic image of Japan called to mind by a travel agent's brochure or by a Japanese airline poster. Usually the image is of a kimono-clad geisha seated under a blossoming cherry tree, with Mount Fujiyama in the background. Or perhaps the picture conjured up by imagination is that of a full-breasted pearl diver in the nude, a house constructed of paper, a bowl of rice with chopsticks, a steaming bath, a samurai sword, some delicate engravings, a single chrysanthemum in a vase—in other words, the ultimate in quiet exoticism.

But we suspect that's not the real Japan. The real Japan is made up of glass buildings, transistor centers, neon lights, American-style bars, striptease clubs, rock groups, television stations operating twenty-four hours a day, and a hundred thousand technicians. After all, the country ranks third in world power. *Vitality, youth, expansion*—these words describe the ambiance of Nippon.

Actually, both portraits are true, for industrial Japan is a slant-eyed America that developed almost by chance after the atomic bombing of Nagasaki and Hiroshima, while cultural Japan is the unbroken continuum of one of the most ancient, tradition-laden civilizations in the world. There, in a corner of the Orient, this nation lies suspended like a bridge between East and West, between past and future, between science and art, between technique and dream, be-

11

tween blast furnace and the sweetness of life.

Kyoto, with over one thousand temples, represents a traditional city; Osaka, with 75 modern post-war buildings, is a sophisticated, cosmopolitan city. Visiting either one, any newcomer would be aware that he is in a strange, baffling, picturesque country—a provocative and enchanting land from which he will bring back the most contradictory and vivid memories.

The Japanese man appears to be clever, modest, and even-tempered; and he possesses exquisite manners. Yet anyone who ever passed a group of Japanese tourists visiting his own land remembers how they strolled about in groups, Nikon cameras slung around their necks. They examined everything with attentive looks, measured gestures, and reserved attitudes—and yet these visiting Japanese seemed to be deriving no pleasure whatsoever from their activity.

Welcome, Honorable Foreigner

There they are. You neglected to let them know the exact day of your arrival, but The Toga Company nonetheless provides you with immediate proof of its efficiency. The firm's foreign representatives must have memorized the file card bearing your description and other vital details. You have hardly stepped into the main lobby of the Tokyo airport when you see them coming straight at you: three men, dark suits, serious faces. Each wears a band on his right arm imprinted with the company's logo: a red circle surrounding a black triangle, inside of which are four large black letters that spell TOGA. The company's reception committee has come to welcome the honorable foreigner. They bow deeply, as one, attesting to the importance of your humble person. Then they timidly accept the handshake awkwardly imposed.

Not one word has been exchanged. The smallest and oldest of the three men once again bows, nearly breaking in two. A Lilliputian with hollowed-out cheeks and gray hair, he extends a card: AKIRO WATANABE, DIRECTOR OF PUBLIC RELATIONS, TOGA.

On the other side, the same information is printed in Japanese. In the top left-hand corner, on both sides, the triangle and disk appear in relief. Watanabe's second companion, Shintaro Tamayama, has the title of Assistant Director of the Foreign Department. The third, Toshiro Miho,

13

is merely an employee, and contrasts strangely with his two bosses. Tall and thin, he seems to be encased in ridiculously short trousers and a tight jacket.

Mr. Miho hands me a plastic box and gestures for me to open it. Inside, there is a packet of visiting cards with my name engraved in Roman type; the reverse side of each card has the same information in Japanese. After flashing a somewhat embarrassed smile, I start putting them in my briefcase, but the immobility of my hosts would seem to indicate that I, in turn, should also proceed to present a card. So I hand them mine, which they quickly accept with much bowing and a brief rattle-laugh of satisfaction.

As their faces light up, their eyes become even more slanted—almost closed—and their wide grins disclose three superb sets of protuberant incisors. All three men wear heavy, horn-rimmed glasses. Their hair, very thick, is cut off sharply above the temples and this razor-thin hairline seems to form a headband. "Welcome to Japan," they say, almost in chorus, and another burst of nervous laughter breaks their rigidity for another instant.

Leaving the airport, I find myself suddenly thrust into a moist and sticky heat which instantly glues my clothes to my skin. The long American car is air-conditioned. The chauffeur wears white gloves. On the right-hand front fender, attached to a heavy pole, an imposing flag bears the TOGA emblem. We cross through a tunnel, then emerge into daylight on a highway which is elevated several yards above the ground.

I look around: not a cloud, and yet the sky is overhung with a mist as heavy as skim milk. A hazy circle of light indicates the position of the sun. Distances and perspectives are distorted; shadows become barely visible and look like puddles. The landscape is submerged in a diffused and stagnant smoke. I had read about the Tokyo smog—I caught hints of it from the plane window as I approached—but the reality confirms the worst fears: air pollution in Tokyo has reached staggering proportions.

To the right, as far as the eye can see, the highway reveals a desolate expanse of black mud. Doubtlessly, these are areas which have been filled in recently with sand and dirt in an attempt to extend the coastline. To the left, a collection of unkempt, weakly constructed factories, buildings, depots, and small, grayish houses comprise Tokyo's slums. Driving past a mangle of telephone wires and poles, I get the impression of crossing a huge no-man's-land. After more than ten minutes of riding, I have not yet spied a single blade of grass nor a single patch of green—I haven't seen a single tree.

Suddenly, I am aware of the silence in the car. Since leaving the airport, the three Japanese gentlemen have not uttered a sound. They are seated, rather formally, in the back seat of the limousine. Their expressions are fixed and they hold their hands on their knees.

"What is that?" I ask, pointing left toward a giant antenna that rises like a haggard skeleton in the fog.

"It's the Tower of Tokyo, the highest structure in Japan. It's a few dozen yards higher than the Eiffel Tower of Paris!" Mr. Watanabe's reply produces triumphant laughter, and they seem to expect you to join in. I respond with an uneasy grin, and continue to study the dreary landscape.

The trip goes on. Once again, I feel a need to break the silence, so I express surprise at the profusion of enormous neon signs capping the tall buildings. Hilarity follows that remark, too. With a growing sense of discomfort, I decide to keep my observations to myself.

An elevated monorail ramp runs parallel to the highway along which the car now moves, high above a geometric pattern of little roofs which seem to have been built one atop another. Occasionally, when passing between two buildings, one can peer into the fifth- and sixth-floor office windows. Soon the asphalt ribbon of highway rises even higher as it curves into the complicated cross sections of other elevated highways, then goes underground, then emerges again. A lateral ramp expels us onto a city street. The car proceeds another 200 yards more, past a long line of drab-looking buildings and barracks, livened here and there by a neon sign. Our limousine finally comes to a stop. We're at the entrance of an imposing building, a brilliant monolith of steel and glass more than 12 stories high. It's the Daichi Hotel.

"Is this the center of Tokyo?" I ask myself. I could swear I hadn't left the outskirts.

Inside, the rich lobby is deeply carpeted. One is barely inside the door when a group of porters surrounds you, relieves you of your luggage, and pushes you toward the reception desk. You register and take your room keys. You walk toward the elevator where you are greeted by a gracious little elevator girl dressed in a kimono. Smiling stiffly, she repeats polite formulas of welcome as she executes a series of bows. Like a fragile, mechanical doll, she seems glued to the car, her eyes fixed on the blinking lights of the floor buttons. She does not move until your floor has been reached. You step out onto thick carpet and hear the muted strains of canned music; the entire establishment is strung with speakers which fill every cranny of the premises with the interminable strains of syrupy Hawaiian melodies.

Room 634 is very comfortable—in fact, ultramodern. Gadgets are all about. There's a wall refrigerator, an electric pencil sharpener, a radio built into the night table, a pay television set, air-conditioning, and an electric hair dryer. I scan the contents of the refrigerator and find a few bottles of beer, a few bottles of mineral water, fruit, rice cakes, and smoked fish. In a cupboard, I discover individual packages of instant coffee, tea, milk, cream, and powdered sugar, as well as a vacuum bottle.

Feeling chilly, I look for a control button for the air-conditioning, but can't find it. Evidently, the management sets what it deems to be the proper temperature. Each pane of glass is sealed into its steel frame, and the windows can't be opened. My room faces the street, but any decent view is blocked by the brick wall which stands about twenty yards from my window. I have an uneasy feeling of being held captive.

The three emissaries from TOGA have invited me to a Japanese restaurant where the cuisine—they make a point of this—is Western style. It turns out to be neither Japanese nor Western—some eclectic indeterminate variety.

In the foyer of the restaurant, all the guests remove their shoes. We enter the dining room where a horrible neon glare casts a sickly color across the low, lacquered table and the floor tatamis. In the corner, two dreadful little infrared heaters are ready for use on wintry evenings. But beyond these inelegant appointments, I notice an exquisite Japanese print and a delicate floral arrangement in an earthenware pot. These subtle touches reveal that I have been invited to a superior restaurant.

I am seated on the floor, cross-legged tailor style, resting against a low chair-back. Surrounded by my companions, I wait in an uncomfortable silence for the arrival of the waitress. At last she enters, kneels at a side table, and gathers up a tray, some glasses, some little containers of sake, and some beer bottles. Then she arises, and with little scurrying steps approaches our table. She is neither young nor old, and makes no effort to appear graceful or charming. On her knees once more, with hands folded on the floor before her, she executes a low bow before each man at the table. She will be at your service for the rest of the meal. Seated there on her heels, she will be careful to spare you the slightest effort, will cater to your slightest desire. She brings and removes the dishes, fills the tiny pots of sake the moment they are empty, lights your cigarettes, does not even allow you the trouble of cutting your own meat but dissects it for you into tiny morsels as one would do for a child. This maternal solicitude is accompanied by endless questions, and by a constant tinkling of high-pitched giggles which uncover a double row of gold-covered teeth. She is attentive to every one of your words. Her joviality and exuberance are in great contrast to the cold reserve of your companions, but the depersonalized animation chills you just as much as does their stolidity.

During this dinner, I try to discover something which will give me a clue to the personalities of my hosts, some little sign of humanity having nothing to do with TOGA. But I get nowhere at all. I do my best to try to get them to reveal something of themselves by telling them a few details of my own personal life. In return, I draw polite interest expressed in clichés. By dessert time, I have learned nothing about Messrs. Watanabe, Tamayama, and Miho, except that they are very proud and happy to be a part of the great TOGA company.

Fake Festivity

Upon leaving the hotel the next morning, I am enveloped by the sticky heat which hangs in the sky, and turns the sun into cotton candy. The air is redolent of a strange slightly acid smell—like sulfuric powder. Strident nasal tones spill forth from innumerable loudspeakers attached to every telephone pole. There is a babel of advertising, and no way to escape it. The little metallic trumpets split your ears all day long everywhere you go.

Thick bunches of electric wires hang over the streets and sidewalks. They block out the tops of some of the somber-looking buildings, whose shapes form a lighted geometric roller coaster. A few skinny trees act as hangers for colored plastic balls, and lend the street the bizarre atmosphere of spurious holiday.

First stop: an electrical equipment store. The shelves hold an incredible stock of every kind of electrical machine and gadget you can imagine: radios, television sets, phonographs, tape recorders, turntables which range in price from six dollars to over a hundred, very expensive stereo equipment, and every kind of kitchen gadget. An enormous speaker above the door belches forth 150 decibels of uninterrupted music.

Further on, there's a restaurant. In the window, you see platters of food with prices on them all lined up for appraisal. When you look a little closer, you realize the food has been bewitchingly made of plastic—a good thing since a layer of dust has thickenened on top of each presentation.

Still further on, I spy a beauty salon: a pitiful wooden hut with a zinc roof. In the window, there are a few yellowed photos of women's faces, a plaster bust coiffed with a complicated wig, and the omnipresent neon sign. The gateway to this shack is an automatic sliding door.

Next stop, a fruit stand. Fruit is sold by the hundred grams (three ounces) or by the piece. Prices are approximately 40¢ for an orange, 80¢ for a pear, and $1.60 for a bunch of grapes. A melon is presented in a straw box as if it were a jewel; it costs $10.

In a typically incongruous turnabout, some two doors away from the beauty salon that is set in the worst slum imaginable, your eyes behold a feast of beauty: here is an ultramodern palace of aluminum and glass. Inside the building, the walls of the vast lobby are lined with superbly woven tapestry and are hung with abstract paintings. Sculpture abounds.

I move on. Despite the lusty roarings of the loud-speakers, which bellow into every nook of the city, I become aware of a strange clicking and hissing sound, something like the noise of mud being sucked up by powerful hoses. I approach closer to the sound. Almost completely hidden by a curtain, I see men and women perched on high-backed chairs at a bar from which there interminably bellows huge gushes of steam. These folks are having their lunch. Each bowl is held up to a chin. The chopsticks dip regularly into the steaming bouillon to grasp a bunch of noodles, which the diner immediately sucks into his mouth with much chomping and smacking. Japanese feel it's poor manners to eat quietly.

I continue on. Soon I hear the sound of a printing

press—a rhythmic metallic chatter. Chinese characters in blood-red neon spell out PACHINKO, the Japanese version of the pinball machine. Pinball, a vapid, uninteresting pastime, is played in almost every corner of the island from one end to the other.[1] Devotees pass up to several hours a day playing this booby game which has turned into a national drug. These pinball stores are always buzzing with people of every class and age, from distinguished-looking businessmen to young couples. It is not at all uncommon to see a mother with her child strapped onto her back. You watch this strange spectacle of people who follow, hypnotized, with haggard eyes, the dance of the balls in which are pinned their illusions and their hopes. When they leave, lucky scorers can exchange their balls for a package of cigarettes, a rubber ball, a can of tuna, and the like.

---

[1] 50,000 salons throughout Japan, 2 million pinball machines

Crowds . . . Everywhere Crowds

I'm at Shimbashi railroad station at nine o'clock in the morning. It's an anthill on the alert. Torrents of somber-looking people glide from one hall to the other, swarm around the automatic ticket-distributing machines and through the electronically controlled doors, and bob up and down the escalators. The first time you see the railroad platform, the spectacle is stupefying. The loudspeakers are screaming, while a human tidal wave is about to crash into the train doors. The doors slide open automatically; the cars vomit out masses of travelers who push their way through those who are determined to push their way in. In this savage mangle, women and children take the worst beating. Inevitably, some commuters become jammed in the doorways and remain stuck there, until white-gloved pushers make their way to the bottlenecks and elbow everyone either in or out. The doors slam shut with the retort of a guillotine. Inside the train, the bodies are so pressed together so that at each curve or bump, the human mass sways collectively like a huge plate of gelatin. You look around at the faces and you do not find the slightest trace of ill humor—on the contrary, everyone looks content and full of a sense of well-being. In this sticky atmosphere, many of the passengers fall asleep standing up, to the lullaby of the loudspeaker which screams out the names of the stations.

* * *

It's five thirty, and the offices let out. The sidewalks are black with people. A Japanese crowd gives the curious impression of a river with a slow-moving, irreversible current —perhaps because of the impassive faces, the uniformly black hair and somber clothes. Pushing is taken for granted, and pushing is quite naturally returned without the slightest sign of resentment or the least word of apology. The visitor is the only person not in a rush.

Kyoto through Loudspeakers

Two days in Tokyo, two days of gluey crowds, incessant noise, and polluted air, have worn me out. I have the impression of life dehumanized, robotized. Since I have one more week before going to work, I get the irresistible desire to run away, to look for that "other" Japan, the one on the posters. So I buy a ticket for Kyoto, "the Florence of the East."

The Tokaido, the fastest train in the world (210 km an hour, leaving every 15 minutes) takes 3½ hours from Tokyo to Kyoto.

And I get 3½ hours of depressing views from my train window. Put end to end the poorest outskirts of Pittsburgh, Marseilles, Birmingham, and Frankfurt, flatten them all out and stretch them over 500 kilometers and you'll get an idea of what the coastal plain from Tokyo to Osaka looks like. Pitiful collections of blackish wooden buildings, tin and tiled roofs, spewing chimneys, large and small electric cables—and all without color, and without any hint of life.

Old Kyoto—alas!—is no exception. From the station which dominates the imperial city, you look around in a circle. Here and there the roof of a pagoda pokes its way out of a sacrilegious mass of cement boxes, chimneys, and telephone poles. As you emerge from the station, a tall, thin tower climbing high into the sky like the antenna of a monstrous snail, catches your eye. A guide explains that, from the top of this perch, the rushed visitor can make out all the important temples of the city without having to take the trouble to visit them.

In the old quarter of Kyoto, hideous establishments have sprung up like mushrooms—nightclubs with Gothic or Moorish facades, bathed at nightfall in garish neon. Wedged between these horrors, and veiled by electric wires and cables, the precious antique mansions, Japan's most venerated temples, appear to be straggling.

You are at the Ryoan-ji to see the most famous stone garden of Japan. In the parking lot, 50 tourist buses parked in close file stand by ominously. The long alley leading to the temple is completely obstructed. Long lines of schoolgirls in black tunics and trousers, with berets on their heads, form a slow-moving, foot-dragging procession behind their teacher. "Stay close behind me!" she admonishes, on the narrow one-way path, as though it would be possible to lose any one of them. They stand in rows of three, holding hands. At the heads and tails of certain lines, uniformed girls communicate with each other by walkie-talkie, for this is a well-organized field trip. Strolling idly from one point to another is obviously out of the question for the girls, and for the private tourist, too, for that matter.

There is a wait to get to the entrance. Then, finally, with ticket in hand, you walk through the main portal. A rampart of school uniforms blocks the view. You manage to climb up on the base of a wooden pillar. From this vantage point, you are at last able to admire, over the tops of the bobbing berets, the exquisite rectangular arrangement of the larger stones which emerge from the carpet of smaller white pebbles—a carpet that has been carefully raked and polished. The overall design touches on perfection, and calls to the spirit to enter into a state of repose and serenity.

But even as you stand before this quintessence of

Japanese civilization, peace of mind eludes you, for a loud-speaker is blaring out with piercing insistence the whys and wherefores of the beauty of this site. Simultaneously, in order to be heard above the loudspeakers, the numerous guides are shouting the same explanations to their respective groups through their megaphones.

Once the guides have finished, it is time for taking photographs. Instructions for posing are shouted back and forth; still and movie cameras click. A photographer snaps, then changes place with someone else in the group who then snaps again, and this goes on until everyone has both been in the picture and taken a picture. With this game of musical chairs going on, solemn vista, contemplative perspective, and any thought of peace of mind have been obliterated.

The Hidden Japan

Sick at heart, you flee this touristic bedlam. You return to your hotel on foot, passing a vast area of sanctuaries and enormous wooden houses. Giant pine trees, their tall branches interweaving like enormous phantoms holding hands, extend gracefully over thatch-roofed temples. It is beautiful—but you must abandon this main road with its uninterrupted flow of tourists. You find another path, to which tormented roots of ancient trees have by chance led you. Happy surprise! There is not another soul here.

A kind of wooden fence surrounds a small garden with only one feature: a bamboo fountain in the middle of a carpet of moss. Admirable sobriety.

Then follows a dry garden. Then, a mineral garden. Not one tree, not a blade of grass. It is a perfect illustration of abstract art created by the Zen monks in the centuries before there was a civilized West.

The third garden is much bigger: beautifully formed pine trees project poetic patterns on the moss lawn. A stone lantern. A murmuring brook. The clear water of a miniature lake which you cross on an arching wooden bridge. And at the end of a flagstone path, a teahouse, lightly constructed of bamboo and wood, with a thatched roof—a masterpiece of simplicity.

A monk dressed in a dark robe and white slipper-socks, glides with tiny steps across the wooden floor, staying close to the sliding *chojis*, the room dividers, made of wooden lattice work and white rice paper, which partition his dwelling. His head is shaved; his high cheekbones cast rich shadows on his face, and bestow upon him the serene expression of a timeless statue. I address him, and he replies with calm simplicity. Soon, he invites me to have tea.

I find myself in the center of a long line of empty rooms. In an alcove, there is a piece of rustic pottery. On one wall, there are ink drawings of mountain peaks half hidden in clouds. A corner of the garden is framed by the sloping roof, creating an abstract one could contemplate endlessly. The monk explains: "A Japanese garden is created to be seen from within while seated on the tatami. Standing destroys the harmony of its composition."

After the green tea, taken silently and slowly, I confide my disappointments and disillusionments. He listens, a tranquil smile on his lips, then offers some suggestions.

Thanks to him, far from the tourist circuit, away from the mobs, I discover a Japan which is everything I could have hoped for: a paradise of temples and gardens, bucolic countrysides. Here are villages without neon signs, to which at night men and women return from the public baths dressed in light kimonos, their wooden *gettas* scuffling softly on the stone streets. Here are peaceful little inns where the hospitality and friendliness are genuine, and not part of the "services included in the price." Here, at last, is the traditional Japan: clean, human, alive, which you can only discover on your own, at random, or on long trips carefully planned with the aid of detailed and precise guidance maps.

This Japan is on the decline, a hidden country existing more and more for aesthetes, historians, and others haunted by nostalgia. This Japan is diminished every day like a shrinking skin before the onslaught of "box office." The

Japan that preoccupies people—the miracle, the Japan of the Osaka Exposition—is the modern Japan which joined the 20th century late, and became in the space of 15 years the third largest economic power in the world. Poster-art Japan is a discovery given only to the most tenacious.

A Hundred Years after the West

In 1868, the Japanese Empire was quietly drowsing under the iron rule of the Tokugawas, a line of dictators who reigned for three centuries, when the mighty cannons of the West began to explode in her harbors, putting an end to seven centuries of feudal torpor. The shock was so intense that it shook the all-powerful shogun from his throne in Edo. His enemies kidnapped the young emperor from his storybook court in Kyoto, and installed him in the shogun's palace. Edo became Tokyo. The Meiji era, "the Era of Light," began.

"To venerate the Son of Heaven and expel the long-nosed barbarians," proclaimed the slogan inscribed in gold letters on the standards of the reformers. But could honor and duty prevail over those black vessels with iron faces which spat forth fire as if from thousands of dragons? The wild cries and the frantic brandishment of samurai swords merely dramatized Japan's helplessness. For such men, humiliation was far worse than death. In the emperor's immediate entourage, a few determined and farsighted men realized that, in order to rid themselves of these invaders who stomped so sacrilegously on the sacred Land of the Rising Sun, the battle would have to be waged with the invaders' own weapons. And they opened wide their doors to Western civilization! Japan determined to learn the white man's ways; to catch up with him, and go beyond him.

An incredible metamorphosis began. No battles and no revolutions. The reformers' oath galvanized the whole country. By transforming the fiefdoms of the *daimyos*, the feudal lords, into districts, and changing their titles from Lord to the more democratic Governor, the reformers found the way to make the lords pay taxes. The richest of the *daimyos*, sensing the permanence of the change, converted to the reform movement, and embraced modernization. They abandoned their castles and lands and launched into business. After centuries of much pomp and circumstance, the samurai caste was abolished. And the samurai were happy to snip off their pigtails and exchange their sabers for scholarships abroad, or for jobs in government.

The Meiji reformers inherited, of course, all the accomplishments of the Tokugawa regime: a system of collecting taxes, a well-structured commercial and banking organization, an excellent network of roads, postal services, and agricultural techniques which were the best developed in all Asia.

Furthermore, favored by her insularity, feudal Japan enjoyed a profound ethnic, religious, linguistic, and cultural unity, and most of its people could read and write. This, certainly, was of prime importance in the meteoric rise of modern Japan.

Under the guidance of mercenary Western professors, the reformation proceeded unabated. The Japanese are apt and avid students. They are enormously receptive and are capable of absorbing and retaining facts with extraordinary speed. They are good imitators. This is an old characteristic. In the 6th century, a quite primitive and barbarous Japan was effectively fertilized by Buddhist monks with the seeds of a Chinese civilization.

"Ah! So Desuka!"

The spirit of the Meiji reform was profoundly nationalist. Humiliated by the concessions that commerce with the "white pirates" demanded, the Japanese concentrated their efforts on the military. They commandered their first battleships in British shipyards. These first iron dragons formed the embryo of the formidable Imperial Navy. In 1905, under the orders of Admiral Togo, the Japanese Navy sent the entire fleet of Tsar Nicolas II to the bottom of the sea. For the first time in history, an Asian country proved that the white powers were not invincible.

The first industries to be built in Japan were of a military character: cannon foundries, gunpowder factories, naval shipyards. As early as 1870, compulsory military training came into effect. In order to train and organize her new army, Tokyo first sought the help of French officers. However, the French didn't make much of an impression. The term "chapo," which the Japanese use to indicate anything worn on the head, is about the only impact the French left behind. A few months after the arrival of the French officers, the Nippons learned of the defeat of Napoleon III at Sedan. Right then and there, the Japanese decided they had not given their army the best possible teachers; politely said, "Thank you very much," and replaced the French with Prussian instructors. The work of a German composer became the Japanese national anthem.

In every sphere, the early empire builders of modern Japan had the intelligence to take the best wherever they found it. From Germany, the art of war; from England, seamanship; from France, the Napoleonic Code; from the United States, its banking system. The same foresight was used in purchasing and making industrial equipment. Silk looms were imported from Lyon; wool, from England. The Japanese required technicians: railroad engineers were brought in from England, mining experts from France, American farmers were imported to render productive un-tried land in deserted Hokkaido.

In 1889, it was pointed out to the Japanese that they still lacked something—a constitution, a democratic one, if possible. "Ah! so desuka?" (*Oh yes, really?*)

Emissaries did the rounds of the Western countries. They leafed through constitutions and observed how they were applied, and they returned to Japan with a blue-print for their country, modelled almost wholly on Bismark's Germany. This choice was not in the least surprising: the Nippons could not help but be attracted and seduced by the discipline of the Germans. The new constitution aimed less at democratizing political life, and more at westernizing the image of the empire. The constitution conferred rights which could be limited at any time, it instituted a two-chamber parliamentary system, with the lower chamber elected by popular vote—but women were excluded. In reality, power remained in the hands of the oligarchy.

After a thousand years of feudalism, could it have been possible for Japan to change its political system from top to bottom? The effect of real democracy would no doubt have been to knock out the country's sense of inner balance, and to compromise her industrial expansion. Furthermore, the very notion of democracy was foreign to the Oriental mind. The Meiji reformers learned the ways of Europe—not for the purpose of adopting their ideals—but as a step toward piercing the secret of Europe's technical power.

10,000 Industrial Spies

At the beginning of the 20th century, about 30 years after her "renaissance," Japan was almost completely ready to fly on her own wings. The West credited this extraordinary mutation to Japanese diligence, obstinacy, and "a miraculous facility for adaptation." Actually, it was the Japanese intelligence, and the tenacity with which it fixed on Western models.

The emperor had said: "Assimilate the knowledge of the whites, and break away from the negative traditions of the past."

That was sufficient. These most-disciplined, most-gregarious people were frozen to attention at the blackboards of their Western professors. They crossed out their past, and allowed no barrier, whether it was cultural, or religious, or social, to stand in the way of their assimilation of foreign techniques. No sacred cow would hinder the progress of a steamroller; no soothsayer would predict punishment from heaven; no witch would cast an evil spell. The strongest were the only example to follow: the Chinese of the 7th century, the Europeans of the 19th, the Americans of the Occupation.

It was imperative to be curious, and to learn how to imitate. The leaders of Japan did not have to resort to tricks to glamorize curiosity or imitation. These attributes were quite natural. In the streets of Japan, crowds gather instantly at the sight of the tiniest new gadget. A hippie, with no trappings other than his beard and disheveled appearance, can create a traffic jam. Bookstores and stalls abound with "pastime" literature. The most inane exhibit draws throngs.

Foreign writers and artists are constantly surprised and touched by the numbers of people who come to hear them lecture. Often, of course, popular appeal is proportionate to the intensity of an advertising campaign as well as to the number of "specialists" publicized. If Alberto Moravia gives a lecture in Tokyo, every student of Italian literature, without exception, will come to hear him, whether or not they have read a single line of his work. This is entirely praiseworthy. And should a Swedish furniture manufacturer organize an exhibit, every one of his Japanese counterparts would be certain to be there, taking notes on everything.

For centuries, the Japanese have relentlessly imitated each other. They *like* resembling each other. They dress like each other, decorate their homes much the same, and cook their food in identical ways. Their way of living is as stereotyped as one could imagine. The formidable amount of advertising that invades their newspapers, television, streets, yields astonishing results among these people who practically have a biological predisposition toward mimicry.

In addition to their penchant for copying, Japanese care little about distinctions between copies and originals. Having become accustomed to a civilization using a greal deal of wood—a perishable material—they are quite used to copying and recopying.

An antique temple destroyed by fire or earthquake will simply be rebuilt and worshipped in, as before. One of the most famous sanctuaries in Japan, Ise, is regularly destroyed and rebuilt every 20 years. To Japanese eyes, new wood is much cleaner than antique wood. The masterpieces of the Nara period, such as the celebrated wooden Buddha of Chuguji, are exact copies of authentic Korean, Chinese, and sometimes Indian masterpieces. The Nippons consider these replicas pure Japanese works. You would insult them if you reminded them that the architecture of their temples, their system of writing, the design of their marble abacuses, their tea rituals, their introduction to chopsticks, were all imported from China.

Up until the second World War, most of the industrial machinery of the whites was plagiarized in Japan without license. After the war, industrial espionage was practically a national duty. Today, the espionage still persists. In Tokyo, there is a school for industrial espionage—professionals in this specialty number about 10,000—and also a school for counter-industrial espionage! During the course of a French aeronautical exhibit in Tokyo, I observed a Japanese visitor holding a pad on which he had reproduced in minute detail the design of a motor which he himself had devised.

Japanese imitations have broken all records. They've made a fake Swiss watch which costs only $5 and keeps good time for about 20 minutes; a chocolate called Tablorou which in shape and packaging is absolutely identical to the Swiss chocolate, Toblerone, but has an entirely different taste; an exact copy of the Dunhill lighter which starts falling apart at once; and "French" wines with French labels, but which are made from Japanese grapes which have been heavily dosed with acids and preservatives.

In the offices of big companies, foreign magazines, reviews, and specialized publications are stacked in impressive piles. This wealth of literature is read, discussed, cut out, sorted, and put onto cards for computers to digest. When this source of information is insufficient for a particular problem, the approach becomes more direct.

Bitter experience has taught the directors of European companies the extent of the antlike perseverance of Japanese who have come to seek information. The Japanese operate like commandos—in divisions. First, there is the fastidious question-asking period, carried out quite overtly in the executive's office. After numerous minutely detailed questions, with every word recorded in shorthand at lightning speed, they get to the heart of the matter. Then begins the slow procession through drawing-board labs and then through the factories. Each step halts with a request for explanations. This allows their photographer time to pull away from the group and zero in on everything that comes within the radius of his zoom lens. Should, by some unlikely chance, a detail be omitted, a lengthy and assiduous correspondence will immediately commence, or a new division will soon solicit "a courtesy invitation to visit and reinforce the friendly bonds which exist between our two companies."

Officials of the French Railway Association remember the notorious tour of the Japanese railway specialists who came during the '50s to try out the record-making electric locomotive "BB." Everything was ready, and the Japanese were about to climb inside the fireball, when they asked to be reassured that this was indeed *the* BB which had beaten the world record. "It is not the exact same locomotive, but it is precisely the same type" came the answer. The Japanese insisted on being shown the original BB. The French complied.

"Hello, Yankees!"

In 1945, Europe was worn out from war, so Japan turned toward the most dynamic model of technocracy: America. Since that moment, Japan has abandoned Europeanization and has sought to become Americanized. She has looked to the victor for the ingredients of success.

At last, the Japanese had found teachers who were their match in energy. The story of this ideal partnership is well worth the telling.

August 15th, and it is noon. In every home and in every village square, hundreds of thousands of women, old men, children, and war invalids dressed in their best clothes. Sitting on their heels, straight up, they assembled in front of radios and loudspeakers to hear, for the first time, their living god.

In a hesitant and monotonal voice, and in the most formal style of language, the Emperor greeted his people. "Good and loyal subjects, the use of arms was not favorable to us. . . . We have resolved to bring to a halt the present situation and we have made a most unusual decision. The exigencies of the moment and of destiny have conducted us to choose the road to peace."

Eyes swell with tears. Thousands of men commit suicide before their wives or their mothers: a bullet in the head or a saber in their stomach. In front of the moats of the Imperial Palace dozens of officers, humiliated at having

failed in their duties, unworthy of the esteem of their be-
loved emperor, commit hara-kiri. The others decide to
"accept the unacceptable and to greet the occupying enemy
with dignity. . . ."

On September 2nd, 1945, on board the destroyer
Missouri anchored in Tokyo Bay, American sailors stand by
awaiting formation orders. A tender comes alongside the
ship. There is a silence, and then the order is given. Japanese
officers in dress uniforms and morning coats climb on board
and come forward to a table set up on the bridge. Behind
this table, shirt-sleeved, sit General Douglas MacArthur's
chief officers. The Emperor's emissaries bow respectfully
and sign a document proclaiming Japan's unconditional
surrender.

When the Yankees disembark, a poverty-stricken, starving crowd pushes and shoves to get a look at the men who
had pulverized Hiroshima and Nagasaki. On the placid
Japanese faces and in their expressions there is no hate, no
animosity—just respectful awe. Japanese soldiers stand at
attention and bow as the victors pass by. Little children
clamored around their convoys. Soon the GI's start to see
smiles and hear "Hello."

"What's this? Are these peaceful people the same ones
who were the torturers of the Philippines, the ferocious
beasts who attacked at Pearl Harbor, the implacable enemy
who preferred suicide to surrender? Is this the home of the
reckless kamikaze pilots?"

Yes, their passivity was as obedient as had been their
hostility. For the first time in its history, Japan had lost.
Their leaders had been wrong. Now the Emperor had spoken.

Douglas MacArthur, Supreme Commander of the
Forces in the Far East, installed his headquarters in the
center of Tokyo's ruins. His mission was to re-educate
Japan in the American style.

A year later, a photograph was to shock the whole of Japan. A tall, strapping man, shirt-sleeved, hand on hip, perfectly relaxed, towered above a small, modest-looking man, top hat in his hand, stoic in his black tails and his pin-striped pants. Everyone recognized the "Yankee shogun" MacArthur standing next to Emperor Hirohito. But no one committed suicide.

The most extraordinary tutelage in history was in the process of formation. "Never before," wrote the former U.S. Ambassador to Japan, Edwin Reischauer, "has a developed nation attempted to so completely restructure another developed nation. Never before has the military occupation of one world power by another revealed itself so totally satisfactory for the conquerors, and so completely tolerable for the conquered."

General MacArthur remodeled Japan from top to bottom. Unlike what the Allies did in Germany, he had the astuteness to govern through the intermediary of the local administration which, in turn, pulled no tricks. There were no "incidents" between the occupiers and the inhabitants. The new master was magnanimous. A tribunal similar to that of Nuremberg condemned to death or to life in prison 21 civilians and military men. Those found "guilty of war," approximately 200,000 Japanese, were prohibited from taking any part in important private or public functions. And that was all.

MacArthur dissolved the Japanese Army, let the Communists out of prison, and eliminated all police control over individual behavior. He gave the country the constitution of a true democracy. He extended suffrage to the women. In an empire where the subjects had had nothing but duties, he established a long list of rights. He gave the Emperor orders to address the population via radio and to advise that he renounced any claim to divinity and to proclaim his desire to be nothing more than a man like each of his subjects. The Mikado proclaimed that he was nothing more than the "symbol of the State according to the will of the people, who alone can claim a right to sovereignty."

The Emperor became an undynamic and non-religious symbol of national unity. He returned to his studies of marine flora and fauna, a field in which he is an expert. He conducted experiments and wrote books which established him as an authority on the subject. Photographs in the newspapers showed him standing on beach rocks, his trousers rolled up, gathering seaweed. Newspapers reported him revisiting construction sites, factories, shipyards, monuments, and museums.

Soon, Japan learned to identify with this refined gentleman and his discreet and unassuming air, and Emperor Hirohito became the peaceful, serious, and confident image of modern Japan.

The occupiers imposed their system of education. They rewrote the history of Japan, and tore out every page having to do with Japanese mythology, or with traditional values or with the cult of emperor worship. Feudal laws were abolished. Agricultural reforms gave land titles to the peasants who worked the land. MacArthur dismantled the great zaibatsu trusts which were the most powerful economic arms of imperial Japan. The great fortunes were either redistributed or were heavily taxed. Wage and hour laws were completely revised, and strong unions were encouraged.

It is a strange paradox of history that the United States, the champion of world *status quo*, was responsible for revolutionizing Japan. Right up until the signing of the 1951 San Francisco Peace Treaty, which gave Japan her independence, the Japanese continued to apply American rules and regulations to the letter. And even since then, America has remained their prime point of reference.

A Bikini for Madam Butterfly

Today, the United States has not ceased to be the powerful sun to the heliotrope of Japan. It is impossible today to be unaware of American influence on Nippon, right down to the smallest detail of everyday life.

The young people wear blue jeans and *ti-shato* (T-shirts) with the names of their universities or "I Love Elvis" printed on them; they use chewing gum, and imitate the twang of the American OK. Their "Western-style" restaurants are 100 percent American, with barmen snapping "Scotch, mister?" as though they'd just walked out of a Bogart movie. Toy soldiers "made in Japan" have blond hair; comic books, sold by the thousands every week to Japanese children, have heroes who look like the All-American Boy, or Batman, or Superboy but speak in ballooned Japanese. The male fantasy of the feminine ideal is a blond Marilyn Monroe or Jane Mansfield—voluptuous, and blue-eyed. The ideal male is something along the lines of Kirk Douglas. And the bars and nightclubs, of course, are carbon copies of those of Broadway or Las Vegas.

In 1969, the most popular television program was the weekly Andy Williams show. Almost all the films and programs bought by Japanese television are American. Upton Sinclair once said "Thanks to the cinema, the world is becoming unified—that is, Americanized." Today, Japan confirms this dictum more than any other country.

Since 1945, the national sport has been baseball. And the Japanese, with the help of American "monitors," have become experts in rules and regulations which have remained a complicated and mysterious maze for the rest of the world.

In the business world, golf is essential to success. Except in Tokyo where there are many Europeans, Japanese take all to be Americans. If you tell them you are French, they consider you wildly exotic.

At Yokusuka, the biggest American naval base in Japan, the town bars carry huge lighted signs designed to flatter and entice American GI's:

WELCOME TO THE HEROES OF THE 7TH FLEET.

HEROES OF VIETNAM, WE DON'T CARRY EXPLOSIVES
BUT WE GOT LOTS OF SEX BOMBS.

NO VIETCONG, NO COMMUNISTS,
WE CATER TO MEN, REAL MEN.

Inside the heroes are seduced with live bait, Madam Butterflys in bikinis, or bunnies in kimonos. Many of these girls have but one dream: marriage to one of these warriors who will then carry them off to the U.S. And that is just what happens to some of them.

It is asserted that if the Americans are admired, they are also hated. For proof, one cites the innumerable violent demonstrations in Japan against U.S. bases, against the renewal of the peace alliance with the U.S., against the occupation of Okinawa, against the war in Vietnam. However, the significance of this anti-American activity should not be exaggerated. The surveys and polls and everything I saw and heard indicate that Americans are *not* hated by the Japanese public. On the contrary, American power and achievements are the objects of genuine admiration.

On the international political scene, Washington is still the prompter for Tokyo. Japan has a kind of political independence, provided she does not oppose American policy on any important subject. Almost every big decision of each American post-war President—including Lyndon Johnson's move to escalate the war in Vietnam—has been applauded by the Nippon Government. It is practically a reflex action. More recently, the entry of GI troops into Cambodia was immediately approved by Tokyo. In order not to displease her ally, for years Japan opposed the entry of China into the UN.

Perhaps Japan would like to break away from her dependence on the U.S. but is afraid to, at least at the moment. The U.S. protects Japan. She is her primary partner in business; she receives one-third of Japan's exports. Japanese bankers, forced into debt, cannot do without America's huge, readily available loans. Japan still has a lot to learn from her conqueror. The Yankees, masters at marketing and at management, still have many secrets to reveal. Compared to American scientists in electronics and in atomic and space research, Japanese scientists are still in elementary school.

Nippons and Americans actually make excellent partners and colleagues. Of all the delegations and missions constantly being welcomed in Japan, it is often the Americans with whom the Japanese seem to establish the best human contact. It is an amusing spectacle to watch a loud-mouthed giant of an American balance his dry martini as he bends over to toast the glass of his timid, waiflike Japanese companion; it is equally amusing to see the formal Japanese face react to a robust American slap on the back. One perceives elements of complicity in the cordiality which exists between businessmen.

Japanese and Europeans do not have many things to say to each other. Americans need the Japanese for a variety of reasons, principally political and economic; Japanese cannot do without Americans for a variety of reasons, principally industrial and scientific. It is a marriage between the elephant and the fox. To date, the spouses have cohabited in peace and harmony.

Japanese Culture, Western Style

Musical products are the favorite programs of Japanese television viewers. Girls scantily clad, and all curves, arch their slender legs to dance a facsimile of the cancan. A tired orchestra gives a curiously Oriental accent to the music of Offenbach.

A breathless singer croons *Only You* in Japanese; behind him, two rows of girls in kimonos hold each other by the elbows, balance themselves first on one leg and then the other, bob their heads from side to side, and raise their eyes toward the ceiling as if in search of inspiration. Then, they suddenly break into large and phony smiles and execute a Gene Kelly dance number which comes off quite helter-skelter.

Next, with a dramatic drum roll as background, a juggler comes on. He is followed by a pair of comics, who scream out their routine as if volume will make up for bad material, which they end up with a worn-out slapstick routine. A barber-shop quartet renders a sentimental old ditty with great concentration. In the grand finale, singers and performers step back, extend their arms Al Jolson style, and belt out a closing number. After each act the master of ceremonies gives the cue for a hand, and immediately sets off frenetic applause and shouts of appreciation.

For "Tokyoites," the place to go at night is Shinjuku, the swinging quarter which stays open all night. Night-life pleasures just pour out from behind a cacophony of electric facades including Arab tents, medieval châteaus, African huts, Bavarian auberges, Gothic churches—anachronistic names completely inappropriate. Behind the client-catching names, there are joints in which sexy hostesses push synthetic sandwiches and local whiskey. The booze tastes like a corrosive. But though I am overcome with an indescribable sadness while traipsing through these specious pleasure domes, the natives just drink it all in. For them, these shoddy attractions are the *ne plus ultra.*

This unconscious caricaturing makes the Japanese appear vulgar to the European. Unless he is completely insensitive, the European visitor eventually becomes quite irritated.

Japan cannot be criticized for imitating Western techniques in order to overcome the catastrophe of World War II and rise to unprecedented economic heights in a phenomenally short space of time. But when this imitation extends to Western manners, habits, art, the results are dismayingly vulgar and fraudulent.

The West's most noble and sacred symbols are boiled down to mush and served up with every imaginable sauce. For example, in a widely circulated newspaper, one can find a famous ad of the Mona Lisa—full-breasted and miniskirted—carrying a tray with a bottle of Cynar, the only real Italian aperitif made from artichoke leaves. If you like Leonardo da Vinci and Michelangelo, if you are an admirer of Sophia Loren, if you've been a *Bicycle Thief,* if you like to whistle a *canzone,* or if you are a lover of spaghetti and pizza, well then, *carissimo amico,* there is still something missing from your *dolce vita*: a picture of you sipping a glass of Cynar. This is the straight-faced text.

The label *Western Style* is license for any kind of bastardizing. On a menu, a *café au lait sans lait* is charming. However, in a restaurant advertising *cuisine française*, a piece of meat boiled in ginger, served with a couple of cold French fries, and carefully placed on a little mound of rice is described as "steak frite French style." To a Frenchman, that's not funny.

In a luxurious steak house, *steak au poivre*—without any pepper grains on it at all—is brought to you with a little plastic bag containing ordinary pepper. No Bearnaise sauce, of course. Instead, there's a tube of mayonnaise. And this costs $10! The most indulgent visitor is outraged.

And what can be said about the "English" sweaters, and the "Italian" shoes which fall apart after three days of wear, and the pitiful pop group billed as "the Beatles of Japan," and the painters who turn out dreadful copies of Western art.

Do You Speak "Japlish"?

The eruption of Western culture has had an anesthetizing effect on another aspect of Japanese civilization—the Japanese language.

A *pureboy* has a *deto* with his *gar-frendo* in his *haikurasu* and *gojasu manshon*. He goes for a *draibu,* but at the *baipasu* he runs out of *gasorin.* There is no *gasorin stando* in sight, nor even a *rest hausu* where he can take his *daringu!* (A playboy has a date with his girl friend in his high-class and gorgeous mansion. He goes for a drive, but at the bypass runs out of gasoline. There is no gasoline station in sight, or even a rest house where he can take his darling.)

This is "japlish," a convenient Japanese corruption of English which has been cleverly recorded by the American journalist David Conde. The wave of "franglais" which so upsets French purists is laughably tolerable when compared to japlish. The tidal wave of foreign words and expressions is devitalizing the Japanese language. The only new words and images to enrich the post-war Japanese language are those which came from foreigners. The predominance of English over the other languages is overpowering, whether it be in words for tableware: *foku* and *naifu* for fork and knife; food: *mirku* (milk), *crimu* (cream), *biru* (beer), *hammu* (ham); beauty products: *haircutto, shampusetto.* Music, politics, science, business, sports—all have been inundated with foreign terms.

A great number of abstract terms have also been "borrowed": *contesto* for contest, and *mudo* for mood. Such words are often used to express concepts which were unknown in ancient Japan. For example, "individual" and "love" are new ideas, as well as new words. Today, the boys seduce their *gar-frendos* with "I love you." Even more curious, Japanese today commonly use English words instead of words that exist in their own language, either because they feel the English has more punch or because it's "in" to do just that.

The pronunciation of foreign words is Japanized unscrupulously. Words are mispronounced or abbreviated: *departo* (for department store), *aparto* (for apartment). When the Japanese run short of ideograms, they write words with the help of an alphabet of phonetic symbols called *katakanas*.

The Chinese learned how to adapt their language to technology, but the Japanese proved incapable of this. Thus, in Chinese a train platform is poetically called "a moon dais"; but in Japanese, the English word "platform" is deformed into *'peratoformo.'* A typewriter in Chinese is called "a machine which strikes characters"; but in Japanese, it is a *'taipuraita.'* If you speak to the Japanese about the bastardization of their language, it will come to them as a revelation.

Japan, it is true, lifted its written language from Chinese. Ideograms were carried off from the Chinese, but pronunciation and intonation weren't. Japanese is already extremely complicated; perhaps the Japanese opted to adopt foreign words rather than render their own language more confusing still. (Learning to read and write takes a child twelve years of study.) The influx of ideas from science and technology was so massive and precipitous that they felt they couldn't channel all these new things through the intricacies of their own language.

Plastic Surgery of the Nose and Soul

In Russia, Peter the Great obliged the Boyards to cut off their beards. In Turkey, Ataturk forced his entourage to smoke. In Japan, Emperor Meiji (1868-1912), having ordered all the samurai to cut off their traditional pigtails, cut off his own, and started a new style. He grew a mustache and goatee, started wearing a Western-style uniform in the manner of Napoleon III and draped his wife in crinolines. His high-level officers had to dress in tails and gray-striped formal trousers for work. Soon, the rest of his court exchanged their kimonos: the men for suits, and their wives for long dresses with bouffant inlays. The wives adopted European hairdos as well. And at balls, they all waltzed to the strains of *The Blue Danube*.

There are many anecdotes to be told about that colorful period. On one occasion, in preparation for one of the year's grand balls, these ladies of the Court had imported from Paris all the equipment they were informed was required to be beautifully turned out, Western style. However, not knowing how to use the paraphernalia, they appeared at the ball with their corsets laced up *over* their dresses.

On another occasion, state dignitaries attending the inauguration of the first railroad line between Tokyo and Yokohama removed their wooden sandals when they entered the train, and found themselves obliged to get off in their stockinged feet.

Today, in Japan, the men wear Western-style clothing, but get back into their kimonos in their own homes. The women also dress Continental style; but when they are past the age of 50, they return to the ancient matron's dress, the somber-colored kimono. The traditional, more colorful kimono is not taken out of the closet except on rare occasions: for certain rituals and ceremonies, or on the first days of the new year, at which time the streets of Japan seem to burst into color.

It is too bad that the Japanese do not wear their kimonos more often. The kimono, with its graceful lines and wide sleeves, is quite becoming to the Japanese figure. It reveals their lovely necks, elongates their figures, and hides legs which are usually too short and almost always out of proportion with their bodies. The miniskirt was a singular esthetic disaster in Japan. The Japanese figure is, in general, not enhanced by Western-style clothes. With the exception of a small class of golden youth in the large cities, the Japanese generally do not know how to dress themselves. Their everyday clothes are drab, unattractive, and devoid of style. By Western standards, an elegant Japanese woman, dressed in the Continental manner, is a rare being.

In the street, the foreigner is observed with curiosity, by adults, and with admiration and envy by the youth. The Western way of dress is carefully studied, Western manners and gestures are noted in detail. The more audacious Japanese have even gone right up to a visitor, seeking instant friendship, and assailed him with the perennial questions: "Where do you come from? Do you like Japan?" Then the inevitable picture-taking request ensues.

Certain bars engage only young, blond boys. These boys serve as hosts to a clientele of very respectable men for whom nothing is more pleasant than spending an evening in the company of these frail, pale-faced males.

Western-Style Charm Schools

These schools abound in Tokyo, for both boys and girls. Young girls learn how to make themselves up, how to walk and stand gracefully, how to laugh and not giggle with a hand in front of the mouth. There are special courses on the rules of European etiquette and manners: table manners, how to conduct a conversation, the art of going down and up stairs, how to sit down into an armchair, when to keep one's legs together, crossed, or uncrossed. Very often, the results of these courses are less than happy.

The schools for boys offer the same hypothetical results as those for the girls—instant Western appeal. Many of the more popular establishments offer cosmetic sessions. Others emphasize manners and a hundred and one ways to camouflage shyness and assert virility in the style of *gaijin*—foreigners.

After the course, heady with newly acquired know-how, these apprentice Don Juans exercise their techniques on the first blonde they run into. They will try to convince the Western girls they are pursuing that while they are Japanese and proud of it, they are not Japanese "like the others." Foreign girls are much sought after, less for sexual ends than as symbols of prestige.

Japanese women have the good fortune to have beautiful skin, firm and smooth, with a natural tan color. Brainwashed no doubt by the touted desirability of the Caucasian features which they see both in movie actresses and tourists, and drugged by the tremendous amount of beauty product advertising, Japanese women feel compelled to make themselves up in the Western manner. The effects are often disastrous. Slanted eyes are particularly difficult to make up with eyeliner crayons and brushes; lipsticks and mascaras, when not used with the utmost discretion, give Japanese women a grotesque Halloween look; hair spray transforms their thick shiny hair into stiff manes which look as though they are held together with airplane glue. Japanese women have an almost neurotic loathing for the least bit of peach-fuzz hair on their faces. They shave their faces regularly, although they do not mind thick hair on their legs.

In order to resemble Caucasians, every year 100,000 people—both men and women—have their eyes unslanted or their noses lengthened. These operations cost from $50 up. "American length, *opeqaishimasu*—if you please." Manifested to this degree, their inferiority complex is dangerous.

The shame of being Japanese is the tragic theme which haunts many of the young authors. One of them remarked: "Our relations with foreigners are curious. Either we do not understand them, in which case we detest them and crawl back into ourselves like porcupines, or we make divinities out of them, and blindly follow their ways of thinking and of living, thereby robbing ourselves of our own personalities."

These thinking Japanese are in the minority, and they are the most interesting Japanese one can meet.

A Feudal People in Modern Times

Dumo sumimasen. Thank you and sorry. But why sorry? The Japanese apology is over and beyond conventional politeness. It does not have anything to do with courtesy, but corresponds to the deep-rooted feeling the Japanese have of being duty bound toward each other. In Europe and America, people are born with rights; the Nippons come into the world with duties. Their education teaches them the obligation of repaying others for everything they directly or indirectly receive: the slightest gesture of friendship, the smallest favor, any kind of help must be repaid.

The simple act of being a client is sufficient reason to receive from the storekeeper the inevitable *Domo sumimasen.* It is a veritable ritual; the Japanese are excusing themselves constantly all day long. The storekeeper keeps expressing his need to do justice to you. "Thank you" because you helped him to make money; "Sorry" because he cannot do the same for you.

These obligations form a complex and stifling web from which most Japanese do not attempt to escape. Individualism among the Japanese is no virtue. As I've pointed out earlier, a word for individualism does not exist in Japanese. A Nippon is eternally and indelibly indebted to the emperor, to his parents, to her spouse (in the case of women), and especially since post-war industrialism, to his employer.

Happiness under the Emperor

After the Meiji reformers "popularized" the emperor as both temporal god and divinity, everything was thanks to him; he was the invisible source of all power. It was in his name that Japanese officers distributed cigarettes and sake to their troops on feast days; that thousands of men left for war; that hundreds of thousands of soldiers died rather than surrender. It was with the cry, "10,000 Years of Happiness under the Emperor," a cry not dissimilar in cause and effect to "Long Live Chairman Mao," that Japanese threw themselves desperately into salvation through service, and into a pursuit of honor so single-minded as to make commonplace the kamikaze sacrifices of the war.

On August 14th, 1945, when Hirohito called a cabinet meeting in the Imperial Palace and announced the first decision he had ever made by himself—that the war would end—his ministers lowered their eyes and wept. Just a few hours before, they had been still swearing that the Japanese would fight to the last man—with bamboo spears if necessary.

Before the war, when the emperor appeared in public, everyone lowered his head; no one could have dared raise his eyes to him. His face was known only through official portraits. Everywhere—in homes, schools, and barracks— Japanese youth was reared in the daily cult of obeisance to the divine person. This kind of indoctrination was much more effective than the propaganda of Goebbels. The fanatical fidelity and absolute respect the emperor commanded produced a very effective army. Not one Japanese, with the exception perhaps of a few intellectuals, dared doubt any word or disobey any command issued in the emperor's name. Examples of heroic loyalty, which would appear to us as absurd, are innumerable. An officer, in a Freudian slip, spoke the Emperor's name aloud, then killed himself to redeem the disgrace. A schoolteacher did not succeed in saving the emperor's portrait from the flames of a fire, and expiated that unpardonable sin in the same manner.

At his birth, every Japanese inherits a debt toward his parents which he will honor all his life. In the doctrine of Confucius, which has profoundly influenced Japan, the child's loyalty to the parent is his most sacred duty. From his earliest age, the child learns to venerate his ancestors, whose ashes are enshrined in a tiny altar in his home. The altar itself is carefully cared for and decked with offerings of all sorts. The child must swear absolute obedience to his father. If in the relationship between generations certain things do evolve, it is less a result of any parent-child rebellion than of the inevitable encroachment of "modernization."

Certain traditional concepts are dying a natural death in post-war, industrialized Japan, but they will never disappear entirely. A left-wing Zengakuren can organize a violent demonstration and condemn his society, but he will bow respectfully to his father upon entering his home.

Today many Japanese marriages are still arranged by parents or by matchmakers. Dutiful and submissive, the son or daughter has no choice but to comply. However, marriage does not free a child of his debt to his parents. The oldest son must live with his wife in his parents' house, and support his parents in their old age. Old-age homes are practically nonexistent in Japan. In rural Japan, elders and children work, side by side, in the family rice fields.

The married women can never fully pay the debt of gratitude she owes her husband, and she is obliged to show it every day of her life. Whether she loves him or not is quite beside the point: she must serve him like a slave. Having legally severed herself from her family, she becomes the personal domestic and often the whipping post of her mother-in-law. If there is trouble between the wife and her mother-in-law, the wife is sacrificed, since to the son, repudiation by his parents is far more serious than divorce from his wife.

The schoolchild swears blind respect to his teacher. The schoolroom whisper of *"osensei"* (honorable master) is legendary. If during the course of a lesson the teacher makes a mistake that even the class dunce picks up, no one dares to point it out. The teacher's words are golden; his lessons, the teachings of the oracle; his knowledge of science, invulnerable; and his image, untaintable.

Never a Knave in Japan

One might think that the Japanese social system is authoritarian; it isn't. The duties, eternal or accidental, are not one-sided. The father is not an arbitrary autocrat in the manner of the Prussians. The Prussians imposed their will on their sons, raised them with strict rules and regulations, beat them when necessary until finally they provoked either revolt in the home or running away. But in Japan, the father does not have unconditional authority. The absolute respect his sons accord him implies, in return, his kindness and goodliness. He is a symbol of good conduct, and is not allowed to fail in his own duties. He is responsible for the smooth running of his household and watches over its reputation. He takes the blame for the shortcomings or sins of his wife and children, and he is required to make amends for them himself. According to his means—and this implies endless sacrifices—he sends his sons to the best schools. No other nationality in the world sets aside and saves as much as the Japanese do to give their youngsters the best quality of education possible. A Japanese father would never say to his son, "Go do it on your own." If the father must make a difficult decision—for instance, whether to financially aid his aging parents or whether to lend aid to a friend in trouble —the Japanese head of family will call a family council, and take into account the wishes of the majority.

The husband is the master of the house, but he turns

over the decisions involved in running the home to his wife, to whom he also turns over his salary at the end of every month. It is she who will give him his spending money, who decides whether or not they will buy a refrigerator, or an air-conditioner, or a car.

Japanese paternalism should be taken in the literal sense of the word, and not as a sort of social politics where charity is the substitute for justice. The same holds true in business. In exchange for a lifetime of loyalty and devotion, the boss is supposed to assure the happiness and well-being of his employee. He guarantees stability and regular advancement. These social concepts are equivalents on a smaller scale, of course, to obedience to the emperor and duty to family. The employer assumes the role of father figure and everything that position involves.

Moral duties and obligations are carried out through a natural exchange. "Do what you like" is a foreign notion to the Japanese mentality. Because the harmony of the family unit is projected to the village and to the factory, that harmony produces a completely homogeneous Japanese society.

"You are not a man; look at your father, he never cries," says a mother to her infant. If the child is noisy, she responds as she would if the child were sick, indicating that his behavior is simply abnormal. In Japan, punishment in the Western manner is rare. Each Japanese learns from infancy to bury himself in society, and to do that which is expected of him.

The Japanese have a mania for gifts. But gifts are rarely bought to give pleasure. If a gift is brought to a host, for example, it symbolizes an apology for the intrusion of a guest.

After a cocktail party or a wedding celebration, the guests go home laden with gifts—delicacies carefully wrapped in pretty packages, or the remains of the wedding dinner. If you are invited by a company to visit its factories, not only will the company pay for your trip and expenses, but it will also shower you with presents. (At times, one might be asked to sign a receipt in exchange.)

Between private friends, the escalations of courtesy can become quite costly. The best way to put an end to the Alphonse-Gaston act is to offer a gift so costly that there is no way for the friend to pay it back. It would be a good-bye gift.

Gifts range from the most sumptuous to the most modest. The parents of a servant will bring her employers presents each year to thank them for having had the goodness to take her into their service. It is in good taste for employees to offer gifts to their superiors. At times, to simplify things, company bookkeeping departments merely withhold a dime from the salary of each employee at the end of the year, enclosing a little note in each pay envelope which explains that the dime was a gift to give "thanks to your employers for the solicitude they show toward you each day."

"After you, sir."

"I think, therefore I am." A Japanese Descartes would have said: "I have a place in a social hierarchy—therefore I am." The first rule of behavior is to stay in one's place. The importance of each person is fundamentally determined by sex, age, and position.

Women are inferior to men. Women should be self-effacing. Their husbands wishes are their commands. In the o-furo, the ritual bath of honor, the husband, then the son, then any male guest, have absolute priority at the pine-wood bathtub or at the ceramic basin. Once they have become adolescents, the male children acquire superiority over their mothers in certain areas. Their mothers will speak to them in a different way than to their daughters. Up until the Occupation, women always walked at a respectable distance behind their husbands. To this day, a woman will address her husband as Sir. She steps back to allow him to go first, and she will let him take the last empty seat in the subway. She carries all the packages; and when her husband receives guests in their home, she eats in the kitchen.

The second rule of behavior is attention to seniority. In Japan, perhaps much more than in the other Asiatic countries, age plays a determining role in the social structure. Ministers are generally chosen according to the number of years they have spent in parliament. No matter how great his talents, a civil servant cannot reach one of the top grades before the age of 45. Of the ten most important Japanese business firms, only two have presidents under 60; the other eight are headed by men in their 70's and 80's. They do not necessarily control their companies single-handedly, but they do lend an air of respectability. To sum up, in Japan promotions are independent of merit; they come for the most part with seniority.

The third criteria is one's position in business. The Japanese are constantly handing out their calling cards. A man with any kind of position can use up as many as one hundred calling cards a day. A card indicates the company one represents, and the position one holds.

Let us look at two Japanese types: they are the same age; they have just met. After having exchanged a few words, they hand each other their cards, with accompanying bows and giggles. Mr. Kobayashi learns that Mr. Yoda is with the Mitsubishi Company, while Mr. Yoda notices that Mr. Kobayashi works with Mitsue. Both companies are equally well-known—more bows. Then Mr. Kobayashi learns Mr. Yoda's position: assistant division director. Mr. Yoda is catalogued. Mr. Kobayashi takes his cue, bows even more deeply, and at once adopts a more deferential tone. The two of them are satisfied: Mr. Kobayashi because he has received the respect he is due, and Mr. Yoda because, having learned at once the importance of his new acquaintance, has avoided the possibility of committing a faux pas.

The prestige of the profession and the reputation of the company one works for are complicating factors. At equal positions, the employee of the big firm ranks higher than the employee of the smaller firm. However, certain professions have more prestige than others. The man who is in charge of a railroad station is very important. Even a lower-ranking civil servant has more prestige than someone in private business. The most modest of pig breeders is a lord next to the boss of a big leather tanner—leather work is not considered to be a distinguished profession. The university professor is the lowest-paid professional in Japan, but the job carries an enormous amount of prestige.

The equation is still missing a few variables which are worth mentioning: the prestige of the university one has attended, which is often mentioned on the visiting card; the family reputation; one's noble forebears. No matter how much character, talent, or grace an individual may be endowed with, only his rank in the social order will decide the manner in which he will be received and treated.

The Untouchables

In many ways, Japan remains a feudal country. The patterns for social stratification set up by the Tokugawas during the three centuries preceding the Meiji reformation have left indelible traces. Society, then, was even more rigidly organized; styles and role were defined by extremely precise rules and regulations.

At the top of the pyramid, the emperor—and in his name the shogun—ruled supreme over the *daimyo* lords, who were in their turn absolute masters within their fiefdoms. (In 1868, in a population of 500,000 samurai and 25,000,000 ordinary citizens, feudal lords numbered less than 300.) To keep the *daimyo* under control, the shogun employed Draconian tactics: border-police toll takers did not allow any movement whatsoever in either arms or population. Spies kept the shogun informed of the contents of trunks and boxes. If the *daimyo* was proven to be too rich, he was obliged to undertake costly public works. No *daimyo* could marry without the permission of the shogun; this allowed the shogun to control and veto any marriage alliance that might be politically dangerous. The *daimyos* were required to spend a part of the year at the shogun's court, and they were often obliged to leave their wives with the shogun as hostages, more or less.

The samurai, or knight-warriors to the *diamyos*, enjoyed one right: to carry a saber. They could not work, and they subsisted on pensions provided by their lords. Their absolute fidelity, therefore, was not only a question of honor, but also a vital necessity of life. Most of the samurai were very poor, and their level of existence was Spartan. To inspire respect and fear was their only reason for being. A peasant, tempted to be insolent, knew he would run the risk of having his head sliced off on the spot. So the samurai came to dominate the other three classes: the peasants, the artisans, and the lowest class of all, the merchants.

Beyond these castes, rock bottom in the social system, was a group similar to the untouchables of India: the *etas*, a contemptible class of gravediggers, leather tanners, and chimney sweeps. The *eta* still exists today, and contempt for these unfortunates is widespread in Japanese society. The *etas* live under horrible conditions in a few big-city ghettos where even the police do not dare to venture. They are a taboo subject. Do not speak to the Japanese about them—you will merely cause irritation. If a foreign correspondent dares to write revealing articles on the *etas*, he may find the doors of the foreign ministry shut in his face, with no way to renew his passport.

The Tokugawas regulated life with inflexible decrees. Theirs was a locked-in, ironclad system. Each family was required to post its status on its front door. One of an inferior rank might be precluded from wearing certain clothes, or buying certain foods, or of inhabiting a house which appeared to be too comfortable. Status determined the amount of money which could be spent for a marriage or a funeral, and even the kind of doll a parent might give his child. To break these rules was to risk serious penalties. This implacable system came to an official end in 1868, but its spirit dies hard.

It is important not to overlook the importance of the

Japanese mother in implanting the qualities of placidity and obedience in Japanese children. Outside her home, a mother carries her baby strapped to her back. During his first years of life, the child is not allowed any liberty of movement whatsoever. He is obliged to follow the mother's slightest movement; he sees the world as she sees it; he hears only what she hears. His sense of social hierarchy is acquired through direct absorption from his mother.

One example will suffice to demonstrate this extraordinary phenomenon: the bowing ceremony. When a mother bows to someone, the child on her back does the same. If the bow is somewhat sloppy, he has sensed instinctively that the person is not very important. If the bow is repeated ten times in a row, he will realize the person is very superior, indeed. If the child finds himself with his head to the floor and his legs to the ceiling, he knows his mother has confronted someone of extraordinary eminence. With practice, he learns to discern rank on his own. When he becomes old enough to walk alongside his mother, he will already know how to handle himself in society.

On his mother's back, the child also learns the complicated hierarchy of language. Speaking Japanese should be a simple task: there is no singular or plural; there are no genders, no articles, no verb declensions, nor conjugations. The grammar is simple; the vocabulary, abstract and rudimentary. But social rules turned the Japanese language into something very complex; there are a number of ways to speak Japanese.

The torturous and strange speech patterns used by the emperor on August 14, 1945. to announce defeat to the country were barely comprehensible to the common man. A president of a company will not speak to a government minister in the same way he speaks to one of his employees. A worker will turn a phrase in radically different ways depending on whether he is speaking to his boss or to the street cleaner. It is not simply a matter of formal speech forms indicating respect as we know them in our Eastern and European languages, but rather of expressions—and even words—which are totally different.

The spoken language of women is very different from that of men: there are words and expressions that she alone may use; certain words commonly used by men become quite vulgar in the mouths of women. Man and wife, between each other, use different words to express the same idea. There are no less than 16 ways in which to say "you," and the ways of saying "yes" are countless.

To simplify this curious alchemy of language in everyday life, the Nippons take refuge in clichés and commonplaces. The spoken language is incredibly stereotyped. It is as devoid of spontaneity and imagination as are Japanese manners. Never look for a personal conversational note inspired by you alone. It is impossible to make double entendres. A vocabulary of invectives, insults, or other vulgarisms is practically nonexistent.

Every morning, thousands of wives say to thousands of husbands leaving for work: *Itte irrasshai* ("Go and return quickly"). The husbands inevitably reply: *Itte marimasu* ("I go and I will return"). At night, he will say to her: *Tadaima* ("Here I am"). She will reply: *Okaeri nasai* ("Be welcome"). Before a budding cherry tree or a breaking wave, the Japanese will pronounce a phrase—always the same—concerning the briefness of life.

The language at every level is automatic, impersonal, and tediously formal.

Japanese society has a pyramidlike structure. The leftwing Zengakuren group is, at the moment, scratching but by no means denting secure establishment politics. In Japan, there has never been a brutal revolution emanating from the common people; all revolutions have involved only the all-powerful minorities at the top: the Meiji reformers, the pro-war militarists, the post-war business managers. Changes have been passed silently—almost invisibly—to the lower classes. This is why the notion of class struggle is unknown to the masses of Japan. The Communist party has made some progress; their number of deputies in parliament more than tripled (4 to 14) after the December, 1969 elections. But their influence is limited to the disinherited, the ex-peasants who have recently moved to the city, the bottom-scale workers in small businesses, and in general, to those who have not yet made a place in the sun for themselves. Japan's soaring standard of living must certainly discourage those few intellectuals who hope that a hard-core, powerful Communist majority will develop.

Ethics and Etiquette

I had the rare privilege of being invited to the home of a
university professor. He was an intelligent man, knowledge-
able about European culture, open-minded. We were seated
on a tatami in a sober, subtly decorated room which
opened onto a small garden composed of pebbles and
moss, offering a thousand perspectives to the eye. Following
a few glasses of sake, an agreeable conversation began,
studded here and there with relaxed silences, on the subject
of the interpretation of civilizations.

My host was gifted with a quality quite unusual among
the Japanese—a sense of humor—and we exchanged amusing anecdotes about the relations between *nipponjin* and
gaijin. With the help of the alcohol, the atmosphere became
even more relaxed.

Meanwhile, the professor's wife busied herself around
us. As she brought and served our fish tempura, our good
humor became contagious, and she began to take part in
our conversation.

Suddenly, I saw the professor stiffen, his face harden,
and his lips tremble. Speaking very quickly, so I would
not be able to follow, he heaped an avalanche of remarks
on his wife in a dry monotone which hardly camouflaged
his outrage. It was as though an explosion had taken place.

After some hesitation, he explained that his wife had
allowed a morsel of tempura to slide from the serving

platter, and had neglected to pick it up with her chopsticks and place it directly onto my plate. I was dumbfounded, and I told my host that as far as I was concerned, not only had I not noticed the lapse, but the matter was of no import to me. Furthermore, I said I was sure it was merely the distraction of our conversation which provoked the "accident."

The professor looked at me with a mixture of contempt and disbelief, and then replied most formally, "You are not Japanese; you cannot understand."

Japanese etiquette must be scrupulously observed. Each person's behavior is ruled by strict adherence to established tradition; the heart and the intelligence play secondary roles. The professor's wife had commited a serious error because she gave the impression of not taking seriously the presence of someone superior to her—a man, the guest of her husband, a foreigner, to boot.

You come away from your visit to Japan charmed with their civility—to you, the visitor, at least. Nowhere else are the personnel of hotels, restaurants, and shops so amiable. The most halfhearted attempt at humor on your part will provoke gales of laughter even from those who did not hear or did not understand your remarks. But the politeness, however laudable and pleasant it may seem, is a mask which serves to hold at bay any direct verbal confrontation. Real sentiments must be hidden at all times to keep from embarrassing or irritating the interlocutor.

A Japanese may feel for you either esteem or contempt —you will never know which. He can seem to approve with great conviction everything you have just said, and then turn out to disagree with you unqualifiedly. You come to realize that trying to converse with Nippons is like attempting a dialogue with a deaf mute.

Or rather a monologue. You expose your sentiments,

your point of view, you reveal yourself—yet nothing reciprocal ensues.

Upon returning home from his first trip to Japan, a businessman may quite possibly receive a letter from his Japanese hosts politely rejecting every one of the propositions he was certain they had approved and agreed to. The misunderstandings between Japanese and Occidental businessmen are innumerable; and sometimes, the resultant Occidental outrage is quite picturesque. While some visitors exclaim, "Marvelous courtesy!", others will rage: "Detestable hypocrisy." Most Occidentals would prefer to be frankly turned down to their faces—even insulted—than to be sanctimoniously led astray.

Among themselves Japanese executives avoid any subject which could set off the slightest controversy. To want to convince someone of something, especially if he is superior, is considered extremely vulgar. But through lower-level company arbiters legal problems are explored from every possible angle: to bring a problem to court is insolent. It is the solution only when there is an extreme case where countless discussions among arbiters have not solved a problem. There are 50 percent less lawyers per capita in Japan than in the United States.

The Japanese affability lends normal relationships a very pleasant placidity, and this in itself can be appreciated. But to confront nothing but rigid masks never lowered is finally annoying and discouraging. When adults bob and squeal with delight at everything you do and say, the behavior winds up as irritating. When you discover that a person who actually dislikes you treats you with even more deference than usual, it is painful. When someone you consider a friend shuts his mind and his heart to you, it is depressing. When a salesgirl in a shop pretends to be looking for a product she knows she doesn't carry, only to return, smiling broadly, with "We do not know that product," you find it amusing the first time—but not the fifth. When a passerby from whom you ask directions gives them in order not to disappoint you—even if he has no idea how to get where you are going—it is infuriating.

When these incidents are repeated constantly every day, you find such politeness absurd. The Japanese do not allow themselves to become irritated. As a general rule, they do not ask information of each other. They know the rules of the politeness game; so in order not to complicate their lives, they avoid every situation likely to get them caught in a perilous predicament. Courtesy is all or nothing; other people's business does not really interest them. Their attitude to anyone not part of their everyday merry-go-round, is neither well nor badly disposed: they simply ignore his existence.

When a fight breaks out in the street and a poor chap cries out "Help!" or "Stop, thief!", no one will budge. When two cars get into a serious accident and a policeman tries to round up a few witnesses, there is a sudden fleeing in all directions. At a Japanese reception, the rule is to avoid striking up a conversation with someone to whom you have not been introduced. To come to someone's aid—an old woman, for instance, overcome with the weight of her bundles—exposes you to the responsibilities of accepting her manifestations of gratitude.

In a bas-relief in one of Japan's most famous temples, one can see the three monkeys: See-No-Evil, Hear-No-Evil, Speak-No-Evil. They symbolize the essence of Japanese discretion.

Outside the Tatami

Outside of this network of obligations defined by tradition, the Japanese is a lost man. Left to himself, he has no idea of what to do. An example of this is the conduct of Japanese prisoners during the last war. During their training, they were taught that they should fight to the death, or commit suicide. Since the possibility of being taken prisoner was categorically excluded, no one specified for the Japanese how he was to behave if taken prisoner.

To the great surprise of their captors, the Japanese became model prisoners. Many requested to be executed. When they were told that no one had the right to execute prisoners of war, the Japanese captives resigned themselves. They did not try to escape and conducted themselves with exemplary docility. Some of them gave their captors any information that was asked. They agreed to translate American propaganda into Japanese, and to serve as interpreters. A few even went so far as to accompany American pilots on bombing missions, guiding them with precision directly to their targets.

On the contrary, in a land which he has conquered, the Japanese soldier conducts himself like a veritable barbarian, with neither restraint nor remorse.

Modern life has created a great number of situations which are not covered by the traditional rules for good conduct. The instant his feet have left his family tatami, the

Japanese can become uncouth, violent, and vulgar. Behind the driver's wheel—often reflected in the reactions of taxi and truckdrivers—he can become capable of incredible brutality. Every year, 14,000 people are killed and many thousands more seriously injured by motor vehicles. The victims are rarely the drivers, but in most cases, pedestrians. Despite or perhaps because of the limited number of highways in Japan, drivers of all kinds are constantly slaloming in and out of lanes. And since there are no sidewalks, children and old people have become the main victims.

A painful detail: Most of these criminals escape punishment. Japan has the highest record of hit-and-run drivers: 26,000 a year. Taxi drivers refuse tips during the day, but extort two or three times the normal fee at night.

On subways and commuter trains, the Japanese are pushy and overbearing to the point of brutality. The relative newness of public transportation allows public conduct while traveling to fall outside of traditional restrictions and manners. Literally off balance, Japanese behavior on these conveyances becomes totally unbalanced.

Meticulously clean in their own homes, the Japanese transform beaches into revolting garbage depositories. Group pilgrimages by the thousands have turned Mount Fuji, the most sacred symbol of the land, into the country's biggest public dump. Every year, the Japanese Army picks up more than 300 tons of rubbish—wrappers, papers, and bottles from Fuji's peaks. In the trains, travelers drop wrappings and waste from their meals on the floor. Pulling into the station, these wagons look and smell like pigsties. There is not a corner of the car in which there is not a pile of rice, bits of fish, eggshells, tangerine peel, wastepaper. On the trains, the men take their shoes off; and in certain remote regions, remove their trousers, too, so as not to wrinkle them. This custom was standard practice all over the country until the fifties. Before the 1964 Tokyo Olympics, a national campaign attempted to get the Japanese to handle themselves with dignity when the thousands of honorable foreigners would arrive. New situation, new rules. On the fastest rail line in the world—the run from Tokyo to Osaka —just before pull-out time, for months on end, loudspeakers reminded travelers that there were toilets and trash cans on board. The rules were respected, and the results were excellent. Japanese stopped disrobing on the trains, and stopped spitting on train floors as well.

That some groups are subject to exploitation is explained by the fact that they fall outside the system of obligations. The director of a company, for example, must exhibit a serious concern for the well-being and happiness of his employees, but he is free, on the other hand, to unscrupulously exploit temporary workers or subcontractors who are considered outside the realm of his protection. Without benefit of a contract, hundreds of thousands of day workers in the construction and shipping industries are treated like slaves.

As for women, social legislation in this male chauvinist society has simply ignored them. At the office or in the factory, she is considered a marginal employee. She is very lucky if she receives, for exactly the same job, half what her male counterpart would earn. The *cursus honorum* is not open to her; and if she marries, she is not at all sure of being able to keep her job. A pregnant woman can be transferred or fired. In the textile and electronic industries, where lower rungs are staffed entirely by female workers, the low salaries and the absence of any retirement plan or health pension has afforded Japan a considerable edge in the international market. A million and a half domestic workers earn an average of $30 a month for an eight-hour day.

The Bridge on the River Kwai

Long ago, the lord Asano was humiliated by the great Chamberlain Kira and bruised him with his sword in a moment of anger. Asano had saved his honor but had raised his hand to a superior. He made up for it by committing hara-kiri. His warriors, 47 samurai, were honor bound to avenge him. With a hundred tricks they managed to throw Kira off guard, and in a surprise attack forced their way into his house. They killed him and placed his head on Asano's tomb. But Kira's murder could not go unpunished. Since they were responsible for Kira's death, the 47 samurai committed hara-kiri in their turn, just as Asano had done. They are buried side by side; and today, their tombs in Tokyo are still the object of many pilgrimages.

This is one of the most celebrated stories in Japan. Parents tell it to their children because it glorifies faithfulness and honor, which are two of their fundamental rules of life.

In the heart of every Japanese, there sleeps a samurai. He is the legendary hero of their films, television serials, comic strips. Total loyalty, complete control of self, courage worthy of any test, honor unmercifully defended with the point of a saber—this is the portrait of the fearless, irreproachable Nippon.

Japanese rules of etiquette are an extension of the *bushido,* the samurai code of honor, a series of precautions and discretions which serve as a bumper and shield against social abrasions and shocks. Nothing is more intolerable to the Japanese than humiliation.

Rather than spank a naughty child or deprive him of sweets, parents will say "Your brother is much better behaved than you; you do not deserve our respect." In Japan, these words carry weight—especially if they are spoken in front of others.

If Japanese workers toil with excessive application, it is partly because of their fear of reprimand. An error can take on the proportions of a personal catastrophe. The guilty party cannot bring himself to joke about it to his fellow workers. His immediate boss would be very careful not to criticize him in public, since that would make the humiliation intolerable. He will take him aside, and express his dissatisfaction with the utmost caution and tact. The important thing is for the worker to save face.

"I made a mistake; it could happen to anyone" is something neither a teacher would ever say to his class, nor a head of a department ever utter to his subordinates. During the war, officers preferred to allow their soldiers to die rather than admit having given a wrong order and retracting it. Such obstinacy killed hundreds of thousands of soldiers. The defeat in 1945 was catastrophic mortification, not only because Japan had been beaten, but because she had made a mistake.

NATIONAL HUMILIATION, NEW INSULTS BY THE WESTERN POWERS, JAPAN JEERED AT—these were the headlines carried by Japanese dailies in the thirties. Anyone with any knowledge of the Japanese character would have sensed the intense propaganda toward preparation for war. It was to save national honor that the Japanese bombed Pearl Harbor and declared war upon the most powerful country in the world. It was a kind of collective suicide.

Many Japanese leaders were aware they could not win

a war against the United States; but since their dignity was in question, the conflict could not be avoided.

In 1924, the United States had closed her doors to Japanese immigration. During this time, Americans refused to receive Japanese businessmen. The official attitude was that the Japanese and their products were to be driven back.

The London Naval Pact of 1930 facilitated the rise of the militarist government; parity among the navies of the United States, England, and Japan was fixed respectively at five, five, and three. The price paid by Prime Minister Hamaguchi for having signed the infamous pact was assassination at the hands of a student member of the "Love of Country" society.

In 1933, the League of Nations dared reproach Japan's invasion of Manchuria. Japan immediately withdrew from the League, joined with fascist Germany and Italy, and began preparing her revenge.

Japanese are revolted by anything or anyone who appears to lack honor. A bum is a rare phenomenon in Japan. If a beggar extended his hand, no one would give him a penny. He would be considered the most lowly of creatures, deserving no help at all, unworthy of life itself. In earlier times, a samurai would have felt perfectly justified in slicing off his head.

During the war, Japanese soldiers in conquered cities massacred anyone guilty of the smallest theft. The arrogance of their white prisoners of war inspired total contempt in the Japanese. "How can a soldier allow himself to be captured?" they queried. "How can men, fallen to the lowest level of dignity, still permit themselves the liberty of joking among themselves or talking back to us? Don't they realize that no prisoner should ever try to escape? No mercy shall be shown savages such as these; they deserve the cruelest treatment." This was the camp commandant's attitude in

The Bridge over the River Kwai.

Given the extreme self-righteousness of Japanese pride, it is no wonder that with few exceptions they are a people bereft of a sense of humor. To them, humor is something paid for by someone else's sense of pride. Irony is unbearable, especially if it comes from a foreigner.

The Hara-Kiri Redemption

The preoccupation with and fear of humiliation has given the Japanese a penchant for suicide. Once insulted, the man of honor in ancient Japan had no choice: he had to die after having avenged himself. In this way, the lowest nobody could become a hero. Today, there are students who commit hara-kiri after failing a year at the university.

What we know about ancient Japan, before the invasion of Buddhism, evokes images of a hedonistic civilization with robust peasant traditions exalting the cult of fertility. The men of primitive, Shintoist Japan feared death. The introduction of Buddhism in the 7th century radically changed this attitude. The new philosophy taught that life was without real value. The new stoicism and absence of enthusiasm toward existence was based on a fatalistic acceptance of death. Honor was, as it is now, stressed as the supreme quality of an extremely stratified life, where only duty defines the place of the individual in the social scheme. In feudal Japan, there was no such bonus as the Valhalla offered to the Germanic warrior. An honorable death was the *ultimate* goal in life.

The Japanese cherry blossoms cult illustrates perfectly the pessimistic perspective of Buddhism: The essential moment, the fall of the flowers, symbolizes the brevity of perfection, and recalls the ideal life of the samurai, pure and short-lived.

Feudalism dominated Japan with such stoic fatality. On the battlefield, self-abnegation culminated in the apotheosis of self-destruction: *suppuku,* the hara-kiri ritual. Suicide, Japanese style, can be understood as a confluence of social and moral teaching that calls for sacrifice of all individual rights to the point where even existence is nullified.

Everyone recognizes, through either the novel or the cinema, the steps which comprise the Japanese suicide ritual: The crucial moment is that in which the victim rips open his stomach, the area where his soul abides (for the Greeks, it was the liver). His immolation is designed to re-establish the order his act transgressed—an error in manners, in the execution of an order, an error in judgment, a betrayal, having shown a lack of courage, or simply having been awkward. It is the dialectic of sin and retribution applied to a non-Christian order. Here the retribution is purely a question of honor.

The Tokugawa regime, which began in the 17th century, brought to Japan an era of peace so rigid, it solidified the feudal spirit. At the same time, it rendered unnecessary the samurai. Since the militaristic ideals of sacrifice and loyalty aren't useful in peacetime, the Tokugawas decreed in 1663 that *suppuku* was illegal (just as, in France, Richelieu outlawed the duel).

The *suppuku* thus became archaic. But the fascination of ultimate heroics dies hard. Even after the 17th century, Japanese history is full of famous suicides: General Nogi who cut his stomach open at the death of the Emperor Meiji in 1912, in order to follow his master, is but one example; and everyone remembers the kamikaze of World War II.

The decline of the suicide ritual was concurrent with the appearance of the *shinju,* or double suicide for love—a more common version of the *suppuku.*

In contrast to the *suppuku,* which expresses acceptance of the social order, the *shinju* is the expression of resistance to a social order found to be intolerable. In its soap opera form, the *shinju* is the double suicide of lovers condemned by society's disapprobation. Right up until recent years, this act was a fairly frequent occurrence. Lovers guilty of adultery were punished under the Tokugawas by death; defiling the sanctity of marriage was defiance of social order. This puritanism is perpetuated to this day under the name of *Fuzoku Eigyo Ho,* the famous law governing sexual behavior which post-war Japan has not yet abolished. It was under this law that the Japanese decided to close the free-swinging bar in the Quebec pavilion at Expo 70. It is thanks to this law that the Western tourist can find his privacy invaded and the unfortunate Japanese companion he invited to his room wrested away.

Both *suppuku,* an aristocratic rite, and *shinju,* a common rite, express the unchanging Japanese ideal or sacrifice. The suicide rate is very high in Japan; at least this is the impression one gets reading the crime and violence sections of the newspapers. Actually, it is the dreadful circumstances of the suicides, ranging from the picturesque to the horrible, which attract attention. Only in Japan can you imagine a woman choosing to commit suicide by plunging her head into a furnace. Everyone has heard of the lovers who jumped together into the gaping mouth of a volcano. Today, it is more convenient to throw oneself under the wheels of a train. But nowadays, the most traditional commit suicide in the manner of the Buddhist priests: One sets fire to one's home.

The truth is that suicide, like everything else, has become Westernized. For many aged people it is the only way left to them for escaping the problems of daily living, especially in the big cities. This discreet exit by the nonproductive has one advantage: It contributes to the solution of the housing problem. (Aged parents generally live with their children in Japan.)

Karate and Zen

This true story took place during the military maneuvers before the last war. During training, an officer gave his regiment an order not to drink water without his special permission. Heavily weighted down with equipment, his men had to march over 100 miles on difficult roads. Five men fell dead from thirst. Their flasks, when examined, turned out to be full of water. Were these men admirable soldiers or idiots? They certainly were exceptionally disciplined.

In wartime, barracks life in Japan was very austere. The young recruits were subjected to unmercifully rigorous basic training. No one ever complained or protested. On the contrary, severity and austerity exalted them.

The taste for Spartan discipline explains another Japanese specialty: the martial arts. *Judo,* and *aikido,* and *kendo,* the art of dodging, and *kyudo,* quarterstaff fencing, and archery—all require rigorous and severe training. The adept in *karate* must master incredibly difficult exercises; they spend hours several times a week perfecting extremely fast and violent movements, accompanied by raucous cries. Their limbering-up exercises are painful and one can, for example, see a karate expert twist his opponent's leg to the point of fracture. In winter, karate experts run barefoot on gravel, and do exercises while plunged to the waist in an ice-cold stream. The karate athlete will punch away at a thick wooden board until it is spattered with bloodstains.

The mental concentration sought by Zen Buddhists is not too different from the concentration required in the martial arts. In both these disciplines, the body is detached and controlled so that it may be used as one would use a perfectly tuned instrument. In Zen, the mind seeks to liberate itself from the spirit in order to immerse itself in Buddha, in the universal spirit.

The Japanese treat pain with disdain, and hold in contempt those who cannot do the same. I have rarely seen a Japanese child crying. He is taught that crying is contemptible. Women's tears are considered "indecent." Showing one's emotions is a sign of weakness. A lapse of self-control is indelicate in that it embarrasses others. During the three years I spent in Japan, I never saw a single Japanese burst out in either anger or joy.

As the proverb says, "Even when he was starving, a samurai would use a toothpick in order to give the impression of having eaten a feast." These pilgrims of the absolute had few needs and were impervious to suffering. Run through by a saber, they would die without uttering a moan. The modern day samurai, the denim-clad worker, frequently skips a meal in order to complete an urgent job before the deadline.

The discipline of the Japanese is collective. In subways, the passengers group themselves automatically with no help from station attendants into packets, inside yellow-marked boarding areas. If there's a red light, no pedestrian would attempt to cross even if the streets were absolutely empty. Tourists follow their guides like troops of cattle. In all the factories, everyone punches in, except the top-rank executives. The unions find nothing offensive about this, for they themselves have a punch-in system.

Where does all this discipline and perseverance come from? The very hazards of the islands on which they live have turned the Japanese into a patient and diligent people. Harassed by the imposing threat of over a hundred active volcanoes, shaken by frequent earthquakes and fires, ravaged every autumn by typhoons and tidal waves, Japan has always been a country in a perpetual state of reconstruction. Entire villages and cities have been rebuilt several times over. Houses, crumbled or burned to ruins, have been built up dozens of times. The most sacred temples and palaces could not endure. If a typhoon or a quake did not destroy them, a fire would. Practically nothing of the original architecture of the past exists in its original form today; everything has been meticulously rebuilt, one or many times.

The 1923 Tokyo earthquake which took 140,000 lives was not the first to devastate the city. In 1855 an earthquake killed more than 100,000 people; and the third total destruction of the Japanese capital took place on March 10, 1945, when American bombs caused over 100,000 deaths and 100,000 wounded during several hours of one single frightful night. And the Japanese are perfectly aware that another cataclysm could destroy their capital city before the end of the century.

Japan is a mountainous country with uneven ranges. Only a sixteenth of the land surface is suitable for cultivation. In the past, working the earth into productivity demanded an enormous amount of discipline. And no agricultural product demands as much work as rice. The peasant must dig little canals to run water through his fields, and in season he is obliged to dole out minute quantities each day in order to keep the field properly irrigated. The work of rice laborers—planting and replanting the buds, caring for the young shoots, then harvesting—does not allow for much malingering. For centuries, the Japanese peasant was accustomed to remaining bent for days on end in continual plowing and seeding. During many a year, the work was often doubled; for often two harvests were made in a year. Since the feudal lords demanded the greatest portion of the crops, the peasants had to work incessantly to get enough food for themselves and their families. This peasantlike tenacity carries over to the workers of modern-day Japan.

One finally becomes accustomed to this collective discipline, to this perfectly regulated and automated life. But one still cannot accept the total obliteration of the individual; one never gets quite used to the impenetrable faces.

In Japan, laughter is a reflex defensive action; it dissembles timidity, pleasure, or anger; it hides pain or shame. Employees smile toothy grins as they are being reprimanded by their bosses. I personally have had the misfortune to provoke this defensive trick.

"Mr. Sakamoto, why didn't you come last week as you said you would?" Mr. Sakamoto's face lights up, and he begins to laugh.

"Please do tell me what's so funny?" I laugh contagiously.

Mr. Sakamoto replies, still laughing, "I had to bury my mother."

Stunned, for the moment, I do not know what to say.

He continues to watch me and to laugh, bobbing his head up and down.

"Isn't that, isn't that terrible!" I say with some hesitation.

"Oh, yes. She was the person I was most fond of in the world."

On another occasion, a Japanese told me, laughing himself to tears, how his house had burned to the ground, and how he had saved his child from the flames in the nick of time.

Three Bowls of Rice

Along with their ability to hide pain, the Japanese know how to give pleasure its rightful, if limited, place. The small pleasures of life are cultivated—the Nippons are not all that puritanical—but small pleasures must not intrude on the important things of life.

For example, the anniversary dinner carefully prepared by a loving wife may go by the boards if the boss needs a piece of work done which takes the husband late into the night. Alcohol is never taken at lunch, but is reserved only for the evening. A business meeting is never lightened by a casual joke or witty remark. On the other hand, the cocktail hour is reserved only for relaxation and must never be violated by a serious conversation.

Things must never be mixed—no sugar in the tea, no sauce on the rice. A little bit of pleasure is sanctioned, but never to excess. To the Japanese, Rabelais is an ignoble barbarian, and the temptation of St. Anthony the hallucination of a deranged mind. An orgy of flesh or food is not compatible with the Japanese nature. Japanese frugality is proverbial. A good table is above all a pleasure for the eye: a few choice morsels, carefully chosen, tastefully arranged in the corner of a plate and delicately caught up with chopsticks.

The Japanese have the reputation of finding pleasure in the most unassuming and innocent things: contemplating the reflection of the moon on the sea; snow powdering the countryside with white; arranging a simple garden of moss and pebbles; composing two flowers and a dried-out branch into an abstract bouquet; drinking mint tea in silent reflection; chatting with a geisha or listening to her sing.

Three bowls of rice a day and a television set would suffice for most Japanese; for the wife, a washing machine and a refrigerator. What else does one need? Enough to buy cigarettes, enough to buy sake to drink with one's friends; the rest—interior decorating, elegant clothes, plays and shows, vacations—all this is secondary. The workers, the executives, the presidents do not have a way of life that is very different from each other. Even from the way they dress, it is hard to tell them apart.

At home, the First Minister of Japan eats the same things for breakfast that the lowliest employee eats: the *miso*, soup with a bean paste base, a bowl of rice, a few pieces of fish; at lunch, a bowl of Chinese soup or rice; and in the evening, another bowl of rice to which are added a few chunks of raw fish, and a few slices of condiments. No one takes much in the way of vacations. Foremen and directors live in the same kind of housing project as do their employees. The only thing that might indicate greater affluence in the homes of the executives would be a few pieces of pottery or a valuable painting. To flaunt one's wealth is considered vulgar. Refinement dictates an economy of show.

The size of one's garden constitutes the only obvious status symbol. Each house has a garden which is meticulously cared for. With poorer people, the garden is very small— sometimes only a yard square—but it is arranged so as to give the impression of being a miniature estate. Deprived of the piece of earth so necessary to his equilibrium, the apartment dweller invariably has a corner of his home reserved for a miniature indoor garden with moss, flowers, shrubs, dwarf pines. There might even be tiny fruit trees that produce Lilliputian fruits.

Hardened by their secular self-discipline, the Japanese have not yet acquired a need for what we consider comfortable living. In winter, they tremble in chilly houses swept with drafts. In summer they suffocate in synthetic materials which trap the sun and heat and do not allow the skin to perspire. They seem to take in stride the noise and the air pollution, plus all the other assaults of modern-day living. In the bigger cities, most of the population lives crammed into tiny apartments. In Tokyo alone, 300,000 families are forced to live in one-room apartments. Almost half the population of the country is badly housed. And of course, no one organizes a march in the streets to protest and demand construction of better housing.

An inquiry conducted by one of the country's big newspapers gave some eloquent figures on Japanese frugality: Half of those interviewed considered themselves to be part of the middle class; two thirds were satisfied with their lifestyle. It is true, that each year since the war the standard of living has consistently risen.

Japan has become the third economic power of the world, yet the average way of life of the individual does not reflect the country's wealth. The disparity between national opulence and the modest way of life of its citizens demonstrates the extraordinary sense of self-sacrifice of the Japanese. It is this sacrifice that provides the key to what has been called "the economic miracle" of Japan. Personal ambition, liberty, and individual comfort have been sublimated in the economic interest of society as a whole.

The Cowl Makes the Monk

The teahouse is an asylum of peace, protected by a delicate moss screen; a tiny, fragile cabin whose naked simplicity creates a feeling of serenity. The only structural textures one sees are straw, wood, the irregular surface of dried mud walls. Seated on their heels, several of the faithful follow in religious silence the ritual gestures of the ceremony master. There is the heavy kettle of cast iron, the lacquered box containing the tea, the finely wrought handle of the serving ladle, a spoon, a little whip of bamboo, and several decorated enamel drinking bowls. Green tea is imbibed with stylized, consecrated gestures.

What does it taste like, this ritual tea? Like its color, it is green and bitter. But the taste is of no importance. The tea ceremony is a Japanese art par excellence; the tea drinking is merely the pretext for a rite. The aesthetic form of the rite must be perfect, for the Japanese have made a cult of form. The framework and surroundings must be worthy of the show; the manner in which the essential articles are arranged must surpass their intrinsic beauty.

The Special Art of Japan

Ikebana, the art of flower arranging, is a three-dimensional art; the composition and color of the whole bouquet render the intrinsic beauty of each flower secondary. The Japanese garden does not exalt nature; it arranges nature for contemplation. It is made to be seen; it is not meant to be walked around in, nor to relax in.

The martial arts of Japan are as preoccupied with aesthetics as are the tea ceremony and the *ikebana.* The art of combat represents the mastery of self-control and the aesthetics of perfect gesture. The man in traditional robe, alone in the *kyudo* salon, poised and concentrating in front of his target, drawing his arrow with infinite care, curving his bow with majestic slowness, is re-enacting an ancient art form. Whether his arrow pierces the bull's-eye or not is quite secondary; the nobleness of his style and the control he exercises over his gestures are the essentials.

With one snap of his foot or one slice of his hand, a karate expert can kill. In championship karate games, competitors do not make physical contact with each other. The exercises and bouts are simulated and the blows stop within a few inches of the adversary's body. The jury honors the most beautiful style—not the strongest or most effective fighter.

The same kind of beautiful, stylized performance dominates the Japanese stage. The *kabuki,* which is the most popular style of theater, is at once a series of music-hall numbers, an opera, and a play. One does not find in *kabuki* the literary imagination of a Shakespeare, nor the tenderness of a Racine, nor the humor of a Molière. The classic Japanese theater presents traditional legends and ancient history. The warp and woof of this material stretch out endlessly. A performance can last as long as six hours. For the spectators of *kabuki*, the fascination lies in the direction, the richness of the costumes, the profusion of color, the incantation of the actors, their leaps, their cries, their grimaces. The presentation is designed to be as far from naturalism as is possible. The facial expressions should be exaggerated and unnatural. The heavy make-up gives the impression of a mask. All movements are extremely ritualized and puppetlike. In essence, *Kabuki* is not too far removed from the *bunraku* theater, in which dolls replace actors. In *bunraku*, the puppets speak, groan, laugh, love, fight, and kiss through the able and marvelous hands of their black-garbed animators.

In *Noh*, the purest of the Japanese dramatic arts, the *ne plus ultra* of Japanese culture, the long-sacred monologues, the songs and dances go on like a Gregorian chant, and touch on a kind of magic. "Atmosphere of mystery and terror," Claudel calls the *Noh*. The formal beauty, brought to a state of near paroxysm, makes everything but the strange smile of the white-faced actor disappear. The *Noh* is a battle between nothingness and death, a sublime visual poem where the incantation of the text casts a powerful spell.

The Japanese have always excelled in the arts. In painting, the delicate scrolls and partitions of the Heian period, and the subtle engravings of the Hokusai and the Utamaro are all sublime. Japanese pottery is among the most beautiful in the world. For ages, Japanese architects have proved that they have an extraordinary sense of proportion, and are in deep harmony with their environment. The palace of Katsura near Kyoto, built centuries ago, is a fine illustration of Japanese architectural creativity. This is, without doubt, the art in which Japan exhibits its greatest originality.

In *ikebana*, in decoration, in theater, in all things visible and concrete, the Japanese have manifested great talent. But in the abstract arts, in music and literature—the specialties of the West—genius is rare.

Japanese music is poor; its harmonic range is limited. Japanese music has never gone beyond its folk and ritualistic origins to become a sophisticated art form. Music requires an imagination and a sense for the abstract that the Japanese do not possess.

Writing, a lost art in the West, is mother of the arts in the Far East. Before the advent of the pointed pen, ideograms were painted. A calligrapher was an apprentice painter; his superior was a creative artist.

The young writer, Mishima, has noted that Japanese literature is, above all, "a form destined to utilize the Japanese language." Japanese literature, says Mishima, has always been much more poetic than expository. The typical literary style is the *haiku*, an unrhymed flash-poem of three lines, each line containing five, seven, and five syllables respectively.

These four characteristic examples of *haiku* poems come from Fayard's *Histoire du Japon*, translated by François Toussaint:

> *In an ancient pool,*
> *A little frog is leaping*
> *And lands with a splash.*

> *In the light of day,*
> *Your neck is the brightest red*
> *My little firefly.*

In the spring, the sea
Always beginning again,
Begins once again.

From his cage, the bird
With sad and envious eye
Views the butterfly.

The richness, variety and depth of European literature are lacking here. The unvarying cadence and surface simplicity of *haiku* illustrate a profound difference between the Eastern and Western approaches to literature.

In Japanese eyes, Westerners are intellectuals. Westerners love reason and logic; Japanese ignore them. Westerners understand things; Japanese sense them.

Westerners invent dogmas and systems; but nothing is more alien to the Japanese mind. It is through instinct, not through reason, that they approach art. Less preoccupied with culture, they are, perhaps, closer to the objects themselves. Perhaps that is why Japan has never produced philosophers, or theoreticians who can shake the world with the brilliance of their ideas and can produce political or social systems that influence generations. That is why an intellectually impoverished Japan could and would let itself be influenced first by the Chinese culture and later by Western culture. It also explains why Japan has never been a country of revolution.

"You know one, you know them all."

A young graduate of Japan's most prestigious Tokyo University accompanied me to the famous Kompi sanctuary in Shikoku. He made a point of stuffing me full of the most detailed historical information, completely stripped of personal nuance. We paused before a contemporary and very ugly piece of sculpture, and I asked him if he liked it. With hardly a glance at the statue, he replied: "It's very well-known."

"Well, I don't like it," I asserted. He looked at me in disbelief.

Then we stopped to gaze at a rather strange and insipid-looking bronze, and again I asked him for his opinion. He immediately answered: "I like it."

"Why do you like it?" I asked.

"Because everyone says it's good; otherwise it wouldn't be there."

Later, for the third time, I asked my friend once again for his opinion on a certain work of art. This time, sensing a trap, he thought he had better agree with me, and he said he didn't like the piece.

That a brilliant student of Japan's finest university holds opinions about aesthetics that are different from mine is one thing. But that he should be incapable of a personal opinion at all is very disturbing.

One of the characteristics of the Japanese, in fact, is

their inability to think critically. This explains to a large extent their passivity and conformism, their lack of color, their underdeveloped sense of humor, the infantilism of their emotional reactions, in the rare instances when they allow them to show.

The editorials in Japanese newspapers are surprisingly inconsistent. Their tone can sway from puerile enthusiasm in one paragraph to rigid moralizing in the next. Editorial conclusions very often read something like this: "While understanding the complex problems this delicate question raises, we hope from the bottom of our hearts that the government will find a way to deal with them for the benefit of the involved parties and in the interests of the people in general." Film critics, book critics, and TV critics worthy of the appellation are rare indeed.

If the usual conversation with a Japanese is insipid, it is because hardly ever is there any kind of a relationship established between the two people who are conversing. You are not Mr. Dupont or Mr. Martin; you are first and foremost a Westerner. And *ipso facto,* your judgment is presumed to represent that of all Westerners. You are not talking with Mr. Sato or Mr. Kobayashi, but with a Japanese who expresses not his own personal viewpoint, but rather hopes to accurately represent the opinion of all the Japanese.

The slightest criticism of his country will hurt his feelings. He will take your words as a criticism of himself. He is nothing but a chip off the monolithic block that is the Japanese society.

When I first arrived in Japan, an American threw at me in a rather disenchanted manner, "Once you've met one, you've met them all." At the time, that remark seemed childish and foolish. But with time and experience, his cliché hardly turned out to be an exaggeration. The Japanese thinks and acts with a group mentality—not as an individual. The Japanese is anonymous. The oddball who, for example, happens not to like beer and sake—two excellent softeners of the communication barrier—is the laughingstock of all his companions.

Their very gestures and mannerisms are alike. When they laugh, the Japanese cover their mouths with their hand—everyone with exactly the same gesture. To indicate astonishment, every last one of them will round his lips and utter, "*Ah so desu ka?*" repeatedly. In casual conversation, the word *ne* (like our "Right?") is tacked on to every phrase and sentence, rendering the Japanese language incredibly monotonous to the ear.

Even geographically the Japanese population is uniform. No human contrast distinguishes one region from another. The life habits of the people who reside in the mountains, or on the plains, on the seacoast, or oceanside, north or south, are all the same. They all wake up, in summer as in winter, at six o'clock in the morning; eat exactly the same things; dress in exactly the same way; and spend their leisure time in exactly the same activities. The homes in northern Hokkaida and those in semi-tropical Kyushu look exactly alike.

The culinary specialties of the different regions are distinguished from each other only by name. A gastronomical tour of Japan would be a dull adventure, indeed. True, there is a bit more refinement in the way of life in Kyoto, and slightly more animation can be found in the life-style in the southern part of the country.

Stifled by social imperatives and by a dogged respect for rigid manners, conditioned to remain quiet, resembling one another, and happy to do so, the Japanese give a general impression of mediocrity. An enthusiastic Japanophile, the Italian writer Fosco Maraini, says:

Individual Italians are almost always interesting, good-natured, witty, and adroit. But as a group, the Italians are often judged to be rather inferior. With the Japanese, on the contrary, the whole is superior to the sum of its parts. Exceptional individuals are not great in number, but the system places them in important positions; the masses follow; and so the machine works well.

The Ant Versus the Locust

The common Japanese criticism of foreigners is: "You Westerners are noisy and talky; you drink and eat too much; and all you ever think about is making love." Indeed, in the eyes of the Japanese, we seem to be frivolous, hysterical people. It is they who are serious, calm, and reserved. They are kind but not effusive, affectionate but not passionate. They may disapprove or dislike, but they never hate. In short, they shun excess and worship moderation. Rather than loaf in the sun, they would choose the comfort of a good bath after a hard day's work. They are terribly bored on vacation and prefer serious things.

I often amused myself by telling my Japanese friends the fable about the ant and the locust and asking which they would prefer to be—the industrious ant or the carefree, short-lived locust. The answer was invariably the ant.

One often hears Japanophiles say that, underneath their stolid masks, the Japanese hide a fervent temperament, a rugged individualism, a passionate nature, and a great human empathy. The examples produced in support of such statements leave me perplexed since they seem to be the exception rather than the rule. In my three-year stay in Japan, I found very little to support this opinion. Compared with other people, for example, their next-door neighbors in Asia—the Koreans, the Chinese, the Vietnamese, and the Malaysians, who also fail to understand the Japanese—the

Japanese distinguish themselves by their singularly cold aloofness. (The Philippines, the Latins of Asia, feel much closer to the whites than to the Japanese.)

This coldness may in part be due to diet. Carnivorous people are generally more aggressive than non-meat eaters. Until very recently, the Japanese nourished themselves almost solely on fish and vegetables, and they seem to share the qualities of vegetarians. Their constitutions are frail and lacking in proteins, and, according to specialists, their body temperatures are generally lower than other people's by several tenths of a degree.

The aesthetic preferences of the Japanese are curious. They prefer a landscape half-hidden in a cloudy mist to one inundated with sun. They prefer cold dishes to warm foods, and muted colors to bright colors. They favor frail women over blooming, robust ones. What could be more impersonal than the gifts the Japanese buy for each other, already wrapped so that they don't know exactly what's inside. Most of these go right back to the stores unopened in exchange for a credit slip. Fruit preserves and fish seem to be the most common gift items.

As tourists, they file in robotlike lines before the spectacles, which offer them nothing more than an excuse for their interminable picture-taking. They will stand in admiration before a tree that bears a label "beautiful tree," unaware that behind them a whole forest is being wantonly sawed down. Similarly, they will admire at length an old Shinto portal, and not notice that the portal frames a horizon of factory chimneys which are spewing out thick black clouds of smoke.

One has often heard that people reveal their true nature in their attitudes toward animals. The Japanese do not particularly like animals. Domestic animals, as pets, are rare. The most innocent-looking cat frightens them. The dogs in Japan recoil in fear when you step toward them to pet them, for such gestures of affection are uncommon. Should you confide to a Japanese that your pet dog or cat sleeps at the foot of your bed, you would be regarded as uncivilized.

I took a stray cat into my apartment as a pet. The next day, the landlord decided that cats were not allowed in the building. I refused to get rid of the animal. My landlord suggested, with a large smile, that since I would not "liquidate" the cat, I might see fit to put him into a cat refuge "where he would be well taken care of, and you could visit him every weekend."

Goldfish are the only creatures generally accepted by the Japanese as house pets. They are discreet, silent, odorless, cold, unimposing—in other words, purely decorative.

The Japanese are capable of cold-blooded cruelty toward animals. The goldfish they are so fond of are also the objects of a little fishing game which can be found on the terraces of most of the larger department stores. In dark four-or five-foot-square tanks, blinded and starving, fish of all varieties are kept for amusement. Sportsmen can rent rudimentary hooks and lines for ten minutes or so to test their skills. They can't be disappointed, of course; the minute the bait enters the water a fish is caught. Its throat ripped, the fish is usually tossed back into the tank, or as sick as it is, it may be taken home to inhabit a jar or a bowl. Of course, the fisherman also has the option of killing the fish on the spot.

On one occasion, some of my friends invited me to go trout fishing in the mountains. After several hours of driving, we set forth on foot across a forest to end up at a fish pond. The guide conducted us to the edge of a section reserved for fishermen. Here the water was thick with squirming trout. The so-called catch was fabulous. Before leaving, my companions threw back dozens of trout, keeping only the biggest and determining the weight of their catch before they left.

Hunting with shotguns is practically unheard of in Japan. "Hunters" have to resort to a very special method to practice their sport. They attract fowl with grain which has been saturated with a soporific. Once the game has been ambushed—this takes about as long as it does to smoke a cigarette—the hunter calmly steps over and picks up his quarry. At home, he plucks the bird while it's still alive. "That makes the meat taste better."

On a Tokyo stage, I once saw an actor cut the throats of chickens with his bare hands.

The Japanese, by and large, maintain cordial relationships with each other, but these relationships remain casual and hardly ever deepen into real friendship. Young people marry because their time has come and they speak of love as though it were a brand of cosmetics. Roughly two out of three marriages are arranged by the families. The first child usually arrives before the first anniversary, and from thereon with few exceptions, the wife is confined to the role of housekeeper and mother. The husband excludes her from his professional and social life. He leads his own life.

The couple speaks little to each other. At night one can see modern young couples who do go out together socially. They sit opposite each other without exchanging a single word or glance. At best, the young husband will nod his head, whereupon his young wife will proceed to peel his apple. A good husband must appear indifferent; if he is too attentive or demonstrative to his wife, he risks being mocked for his lack of virility.

Basically misogynistic, the Japanese men prefer to form their friendships with other men. Although they are faithful friends, their relationships are severely limited. A schoolboy or a worker will consider all his peers pals; yet friendship, in the true sense of the word, is rare. The Japanese do not confide in each other; their ties are limited in fact to social obligations. Personal relations play a greater role in business and politics in Japan than they do in the West. The foreigner should note that before he can establish a successful business relationship he must first make friendly overtures.

In Japan it would be difficult for a chemist in one firm to have a friend who is a chemist in a rival firm. It would not be looked upon well. Faithfulness between friends would disappear if it interfered with business. I heard of a case of an engineer whose close friend was the object of a flagrant injustice. He could have defended his friend, but he did not. Why? "Because it isn't done," he explained to me, "even for one's closest friend." The unwritten laws of collective solidarity take precedence over those of friendship.

This living in an emotional vacuum contaminates the Japanese character. It explains the emptiness of their conversations, the blandness of their automatonlike expressions. It explains, too, many of their social ways—the errantry of the husbands, the sake cult, the enslavement to television. No other people in the world spend as much time glued to the tiny television screen as do the Japanese.

Without *real* friends, and deprived of true feminine companionship, the Japanese remains very much alone most of his life. After an evening spent with friends, after having eaten, drunk, laughed, and talked, he is *sabishi;* an impossible word to translate which signifies at once: alone, sad, nostalgic, and melancholic. He is *sabishi* beneath the blooming cherry trees, *sabishi* on holidays, *sabishi* when he walks through a wood or garden. It is small wonder then, that the Japanese narcotize themselves in front of the TV set.

During the last war, Japanese soldiers tied cadavers to the backs of prisoners before abandoning them in forests. In the cities of Japan today, a devitalized people also seem to be dragging cadavers on their backs, cadavers which represent the renunciation of an individual life.

A Hundred Million Pals

Stripped of his social trappings, the Japanese is vulnerable, and begins to be human, somewhat tender. He may not allow his feelings to show, but he reacts. He may be cold, but he is sensitive, even though the sensitivity be passive. Try to get him to share your tastes, your passions, or your ideas and you'll find his reactions half-hearted. But should you slip in your attention or your manners toward him, he will be deeply hurt and will suffer secretly.

To the Japanese, the best moment of his day is his evening *o-furo*, or traditional hot bath. There are hundreds of spas where the natural hot water, or the burning mud or sand, provide supreme joy for countless vacationers. Where does the Japanese get his love for the *o-furo*? First of all, the Japanese attach a great importance to the cleanliness of the body. Then, in houses without central heating, the *o-furo* is a way to soak up heat before retiring. But the honorable bath has another virtue: It relaxes one from all the frustrations of society, from the daily aggressions of life in the city. The burning hot water, often intolerable for the non-initiated, desensitizes and heals the charred nerves. The heat rises to the brain, and acts as a soporific.

Japanese find happiness in groups. One might say that Japanese exist only collectively. There is something primitive about the Japanese gregariousness. Rather than a solitary walk or an outing with one's family, the Japanese pre-

fer a group excursion organized by a company, a cooperative, or an association. By the dozens, if not the tens of
dozens, they go off in convoys to climb in single lines up
mountains, to picnic in garden restaurants which can serve
up to 10,000 people at once, to visit the temples of Kyoto
(sometimes waiting a whole day in line for a drink), or to
buy the indispensable souvenir. They will fill entire hotels,
bathe in packs, and dine in immense banquetlike dining
halls. And to give the day a happy ending, like well-behaved
schoolchildren, they will all sing together from song sheets.
Very few will dare to go off and explore their country on
their own rather than resort to the incredibly mechanical
and precise organized tour.

The Japanese will leave a quiet spot to move to a place
a few hundred yards away, to enjoy the delights of communal experience. One encounters testimonials to this
togetherness every Monday in the daily press. Enthusiastic
headlines and frightful photographs report: ON MOUNT FUJI,
20,000 CLIMBERS ON SUNDAY. ON A BEACH OBSERVING THE
MIGRATION OF BIRDS, 500 PHOTOGRAPHERS SHOULDER TO
SHOULDER. AT THE OLYMPIC POOL OF YOYOCI, 10,000 SWIM-
MERS. ON THE BEACH OF ZUSHI OUTSIDE OF TOKYO (roughly
500 yards long and 50 yards wide), 320,000 BATHERS.

The total absence of privacy does not seem to bother in
the slightest the myriad couples who get married in factories, exchanging their vows of fidelity alongside the building cranes, say, of the giant Kobe Steel Company. They go
away in groups of several dozen couples on organized
honeymoons. They spend their entire honeymoons *en groupe,*
separating into couples only at night, in front of their
respective rooms. Everything is arranged for their happiness, including a breakfast served later than the usual one,
featuring toast served in the shape of little hearts.

I asked a young woman what she had done during her

vacation, and she answered that she had gone skiing.

"Alone?"

"No, with friends."

"How many friends?"

"About a hundred." A candid and typical reply.

In Japan, all the people in the group to which one belongs are considered friends. Thus, carrying it to its logical conclusion, 100 million Japanese are all pals.

This aspect of group psychology prevails everywhere. Between two unknown and identical highway restaurants, a Japanese will automatically choose the one in which there are the most people. This collective taste makes the Japanese susceptible to fads, to the delight of manufacturers and advertisers who can constantly promote new products. A few years ago, there was a run on collecting semi-precious stones on geegaws to decorate cars, and on plastic Walt Disney animals. The electronics industry comes out every month with new gadgets, which the Japanese, confirmed gadgetomaniacs, buy up avariciously.

Skiing, a sport which in 1960 was practiced by only several thousand young people, has become a national pastime. Seven to eight million skiers are on the slopes every year. Today, there is hardly a student who has not gone skiing at least once in his life. And baseball, virtually unknown before the Occupation, is another hugely popular sport. The baseball bat, which everyone knows how to handle, has now replaced the samurai saber.

In the rural areas, the farm work is almost always done collectively. The majority of professionals work in associate groups, a trend which, as a matter of fact, has recently been spreading in Europe. But in Japan, even creative artists work collectively, not by sharing their separate ideas with each other as one might think, but by getting together to collectively find an idea. As for actors and directors, they are almost all employed by large movie companies and paid by the month rather than for a project. The exercise of collective imagination in the creative arts sometimes yields questionable results.

Japan is a country of Stakhanovite collectivism. The Japanese gives the best of himself to his vocation. His self-control, his implacable sense of discipline, his immutable loyalty, the magnetic appeal that communal effort has for him, all these make him the best salaried worker in the world. Taken individually, however, the Japanese are not workhorses. On the contrary, when one visits offices and workshops one is surprised at the calm, unharried atmosphere. Work is often interrupted for a cup of tea or some small talk. The most minor problems are worked out in discussion. The productivity rate of the Japanese workers is inferior to that of the Western worker. But the Japanese thinks and works for the group; consequently, the sum of work produced in Japan is superior to that produced in the West. We often take two steps backward for every step forward. Our individuals, with their personalities and their original ideas, often slow up the steady step of production. In Japan, work progression is continuous. An employee thinks less of his own interests than he does of those of the company and society. His greatest ambition is to be appreciated and estimated by his superiors, to contribute to the prosperity of his company and his country.

Buddha, Muhammad, and Jesus Christ

The two principal religions in Japan, Shintoism and Buddhism, are not practiced in the way that we understand religions to be, and do not, for example, impose regular attendance at religious services. Of all the non-communist countries of the world, Japan is, by far, the least religious. In 1960, when asked "Do you practice a religion?" 88 percent of those questioned answered negatively. A more recent survey indicated that only 3 percent practice any religion (as compared to 50 percent in Holland, 40 percent in England, and 38 percent in the United States). Among the 3 percent who do practice a religion, it is interesting to note that many are Christians—Protestants and Catholics.

Many scholars maintain that the people of Japan are mystical, and that this taste for mysticism explains the success in Japan of foreign religions, principally Indian Buddhism, Chinese Zen, and with the advent of missionaries in the 16th century, Christianity. They explain that the Japanese need for mystery and for a god was anesthetized by the industrial progress imposed on postwar Japan, but that the need was not annihilated entirely. The truth, as I see it, is quite different.

Shintoism, the original religion, is *the* religion of the Japanese; the Japanese are the only ones, in fact, who practice it. Shintoism has remained in its ancient, primitive, and original form. Rather than a mystic force, Shintoism constitutes a kind of collective self-defense against the assaults of Nature. It is an ensemble of rites, many of a purifying nature. Obeisance is paid to thousands of good and evil genies; they are the spirits of Nature and the spirits of one's ancestors. Anything capable of capturing the presence of a spirit—a fountain, a huge tree, a rock, a volcano—is a Shinto sanctuary. There are 600,000 of these sanctuaries sprinkled all over the country, of which 87,000 are formal temples.

This religion, without any real spiritualism, was broken up through the years into a large number of sects, 160 of which still exist but without strong following, since Shintoism readily allowed itself to be absorbed into Buddhism or to be used for political ends. In the 17th century, after tacking on to it a bit of Chinese Confucianist morality, the Tokugawas brought Shintoism back into fashion, in order to make it an instrument of national conscience and cohesion. After the Meiji restoration, Shintoism became a state religion. Combining Japanese mythology with the cult of the emperor, the religion became a catalyst for nationalism, and, with the war, a source of aggression by the "chosen race."

Banished from the Japanese constitution in 1945, Shintoism became powerless. Sightseeing trips and religious holidays are the rare occasions on which Japanese might go to a Shinto temple. A Shinto priest is hardly ever called upon, except perhaps to add solemnity to certain ceremonial occasions: the cornerstone laying for a skyscraper, or the christening of an oil tanker. At times, the Shinto priest might be asked to bless a newborn child, or bless newlyweds, or to chase away some evil spirits with a shake of his paper baton. However, funerals remain the exclusive domain of Buddhist monks.

Compared with Buddhism, Shintoism, an animistic religion without doctrine or moral, carries little weight. In the second half of the 6th century, Korean and Chinese monks spread the religion of India in Japan. This religion caught on quickly and soon annexed Shintoism. The Japanese elite were immediately attracted to the highly intellectual philosophy of Buddhism, and the Japanese masses were fascinated by the color and picturesqueness of Buddhist ceremonies. But Buddhism was, above all, an expression of the civilization of the Chinese. The Japanese masses quickly adopted a popularized Buddhism, and these sects vulgarized the religion by promising Nirvana to all good Japanese who spent their lives invoking the name of Buddha.

At the end of the 12th century, the upper classes were seduced by a new form of Buddhism from China—Zen. Zen aims for harmony with the universe. Zen rejects logic and practical learning, and requires an extreme degree of mental concentration. This form of religion is quite suited to the Japanese mentality.

In the 16th century, Saint Francis Xavier arrived in Kyushu. He represented an unknown civilization, one more advanced than the Japanese, and his mission met with instant success. In two years, he converted the Japanese, almost en masse. Thirty years after his departure, there were 150,000 Christians; a hundred years later there were 300,000 Christians in Japan. Without the anathema imposed by the Tokugawas and the subsequent persecution of the Christians, Japan would perhaps have become a Christian country. The Japanese propensity for conversion being what it is, it could well have invaded the religious sphere, as well as the intellectual and technical.

Religion in Japan was never really the source of a vibrant faith, a mystical élan, a universal morality. More than a spiritual ideal, religion constituted a style of life.

What remains of religion in Japan today? Not very

much. Religion plays no vital role. The country is not atheistic; it is completely agnostic. Many Japanese will tell you that they are both Shintoist and Buddhist. They are born Shinto, and they die Buddhist. There are some sects which combine Christianity and Buddhism. One sect, still active, reveres Buddha, Moses, Muhammad, and Christ all at the same time.

Preaching in Japan is an unrewarding task for Christian missionaries. Those whom I have met relate that they have suffered from the worst possible obstacle: total indifference. "They listen to us politely, smilingly, but they never come back. If some of them do come back, it is only because they do not want to hurt our feelings."

The questions of God, the soul, immortality, good, and evil do not preoccupy most Japanese. Religious beliefs and practices have been relegated to the realms of folklore and tourism. Temples survive from the offerings of tourists. In the spring, when the cherry blossoms are in flower, the temples organize colorful celebrations in honor of a divinity, or torchlight processions, and Saturnalian races for scantily clad young men.

Production-Line Abortions

Religion, therefore, was never an obstacle to modernization in Japan. The Japanese have no divinely ordained social stratification which they must respect, no church with either political or social power, no rabbis, no imams, no bishops, and no Sadducees to pacify.

The abolition of social castes, and the institution of divorce and abortion laws, were not contested by any organized system of morality. The rapid institution of birth control is an excellent example of the advantage an amoral society sustains in the race toward progress.

Infanticide and abortion were common practices before the Meiji regime. In the Japanese language, "infanticide" and "deweeding" are the same words. The population maintained a natural balance through these practices. At the end of the 19th century, the reformers listened to the reprobations of foreigners, and began outlawing these procedures. Of course, they might have calculated that the resultant rise in population would coincide with a hoped-for expansion of industrial growth. Japan, parents were told, needed 100 million supermen.

In 1868, the population of Japan was 25 million; in 1918, it had risen to 50 million. Although the war had killed 3 million, at the hour of their defeat in World War II, the Japanese were 70 million strong. The economy had been destroyed; rice was scarce; and 6 million "conquerors" were returning home to put an even greater strain on the economy. And then, the famous baby boom occurred. In three years, from 1947 to 1949, more than 8 million little Nippons were born. To curb this avalanche the government once more legalized abortion, and no one was opposed. In 1955, the birth rate had fallen from 34 births per 1000 (in 1947), to less than 20 per 1000. The danger of over-population had been averted. Today, the birth rate is about 17 per 1000, one of the lowest in the world; the average family has only two children.

In 1969, there were 1,900,000 births in Japan, and just as many abortions. At least one abortion took place every 15 seconds. A woman went for an abortion as casually as she would have gone to the dentist. Gynecologists practically operated in assembly lines.

Nowadays, a great many Japanese women have themselves sterilized after their first or second child. Contraceptives are sold openly in drugstores. The pill is gaining ground, and consequently, abortions are becoming less frequent. This wholesale acceptance of birth control, unique in world history, has been so successful that the government, faced with a possible depletion of the national work force, is considering a change of policy.

When the Samurai Fall in Love

On the screen, technicolor has almost completely replaced black and white. An erotic scene unfolds:

Naked women, their feet tied with rope, hang from the ceiling. Other women are attached to gallows or lie on torture benches. A man enters. Fear illuminates all the female faces. The actor casts a glance of contempt and hate over the strange assembly. He moves from one body to another, eliciting a symphony of groans. He sinks his teeth into the breast of one of the victims, while he whips another.

The actor stops in front of his chosen prey. She is stretched out on a table. He digs into her flesh with his nails. One can see great pain on the face of the woman, also great pleasure. With her eyes, she appeals to her torturer and offers herself. The camera stands firm throughout the preliminaries, then zooms into the expression of the victim, which is convulsed with fear and then bathed in ecstasy.

End of erotic sequence.

No one in the movie house laughs. A religious silence reigns. The audience is enthralled, enchanted. There are many men, of course, and adolescents whose suspended gum-chewing begins again in earnest after this sequence. There are also couples. There are always young couples in attendance in the cinemas that show erotic films which abound in Tokyo and in all the cities of Japan. The "erotico-production" is the temple of sex education. Or at least, attendance at several such productions is a necessary ritual at the dawn of an affair or of a life together.

The message is obvious: "The torturer is me; it's every Japanese man. I am a latent sadist, and your role is clear: to be a subjugated woman, body and soul in service to your master, and along with your suffering to gain the compensation of ecstatic pleasure."

Sado-Masochistic Delirium

The character of the Japanese people can be perceived in these erotic productions, as well as in the other popular film productions, in cartoons, and in all mass-appeasing entertainment. In the U.S., the archetypal film hero is the adventurer yearning to do justice. In Russia, the hero is an idealist and a romantic. In France, film heroes are clever operators and libertines. In Japan, the heroes are tough, violent men.

The reader is familiar with this violence in the Japanese films he has seen. He will remember the savagery of *Naked Island* long after the beauty of its scenes has faded from memory; for example, the violent and unexpected slap a peasant gives his wife for spilling a bucket of water. Or the various versions of rape of *Rashomon;* or the outpouring of blood in *Gates of Hell;* and the cruelty in *Stories of the Half Moon.* If it is true that sexual conduct reveals one's true nature, sex in Japan, as it is manifested commercially, most often betrays extreme violence.

The famous Japanese prints, reproduced by Europeans, emit subtly toned hints as to the nature of Japanese eroticism. Examined closely, these prints and erotic collections, known as *shounga,* prove most instructive. In the great majority, the love actions and expressions are harshly drawn. In the past, timid parents would slip copies of these prints into the kimono sleeves of their about-to-be-married daughters to inform them of the sexual practices and desires of men. Even in the most subtle depictions, the act of love borders on rape.

The bombing of Hiroshima, and the defeat in the war traumatized the Japanese. The ancient value system crumbled. In the spiritual wasteland that ensued, there was nothing left but the cult of the golden calf. Moral restraints were shattered. Sex, highly commercialized, invaded the streets. Today, Hiroshima is one of the most depraved of Japanese cities.

Violence is encountered everywhere—in the cinema, in the cheap magazines that everyone, young or old, vulgar or dignified, seems to read, on seven television channels—everything is astonishingly bloody. And when the subject is sex, the flagrant sado-masochism stuns even the most sophisticated and sympathetic foreign visitor.

The cruel scene described at the beginning of this chapter is but one example among thousands of this sado-masochism, and it is one of the less offensive because it is patently unreal. In the erotic productions turned out by the thousands, and shown in special cinemas which are open round the clock, the cruelty is direct.

In the ordinary cinema or on TV, physical or mental sadism is a bit more subtle. But in comic books which are sold by the millions each year, the bad taste can touch on the fantastic. On every page, the woman is brutalized, tortured, stabbed by a samurai saber, pierced by a dagger, humiliated. In these stories the female is frequently vulgarly depicted with the head of a woman and the body of an octopus, elephant, snake, or pig.

Let's risk an explanation: In Japan, violence in every form—from the most subtle to the most crass, and especially violence in sex—is at once the compensation for, and the admission of, impotence.

The Man-Child

In few countries is everyday life as strict and stifling as it is in Japan. For the Japanese, the relief of confiding in friends is taboo, and the humiliations, defeats, frustrations mount up. Some kind of outlet is required. Escape is found in night life, alcohol (the Japanese drink a lot), and sex. At least a few times a week, after leaving work and before going home where boredom awaits, the average Japanese male will indulge himself in a bit of a spree. If he can afford it, he does this every day.

His spree might begin, for example, with a turn at the pinball machines. After that, it's the baths—either Japanese, Finnish, Roman, or Turkish style—where he undresses, vaporizes, washes, bathes, gets massaged either "totally," or "specially," depending on the extras he requests. Then he is swathed, perfumed, and dressed by a young girl who wears a provocative minimum. All this takes between 30 and 45 minutes. And now, on to the next diversion.

He goes looking for a bar, where he will find a bit of gaiety, and down a few glasses of sake or beer. A hostess, dressed in a kimono, or dressed Western style, or hardly dressed at all, depending on the type of establishment he has chosen, will invariably come, sit next to him, and attempt to distract him. For each customer, it will be the same conversation, the same jokes, the same little games. After the drinks, there'll be some close dancing, and some, usually unsuccessful, attempts at seduction. That's it.

The most frustrated are not content with this mild diversion. Needing, but lacking, real outlets for their rage and aggression, they resort to fantasy sex and violence in the cinema, or they might console themselves with a *stripout-tisou*, where they can enjoy witnessing the degradation of women who need to earn their living in this way. In most clubs, the striptease dancers take off their clothes without grace or eroticism, and without much dancing either, for that matter. The name of the game is crude voyeurism, in the raw and to the point. In the blink of an eye, the girls are completely "nudo"; exhibit themselves in detail, allow themselves to be touched anywhere and everywhere, perform lesbian or masturbatory routines, and then it's all over. Most of the men will trot home, overpowered with the spectacle of women, and confirmed in their own impotence.

This impotence, manifested in all the Japanese erotic art and literature, is really at the basis of all the violence, for is not violence only a cover-up for weakness? The monstrous sadism and brutality hide the fact that the Japanese male actually suffers from an inferiority complex with regard to women.

Male adolescents, and even adults, manifest the confusion of schoolboys when a woman approaches. As bachelors, they spend their free time among themselves, without women. When they marry, they neglect their wives, but do not seek mistresses. Are they, then, insensitive to womanly charm? I don't think so; perhaps they are embarrassed by a women because she dominates the man.

Men who want to pursue their fantasies more realistically are not numerous. Prostitution has been forbidden in Japan since April 1, 1958. It has gone underground, of course, but it remains limited. However, one third of the women between the ages of eighteen and forty earn their livelihood, often honorably, without becoming "instruments of pleasure," by catering to the male need for diversion.

There are no more than a few hundred genuine geisha left, mostly maintained through the expense accounts of the big companies. The training geisha receive renders them too costly for all but a few wealthy clients. An evening hostessed by geisha can run as high as $100 or $200 per person. A prospective geisha enters her training in adolescence; during most of her life, unless a wealthy "protector" liberates her, she will be paying back the "Madame Mother" who has educated her. Undertaking the "protection" of a geisha is exorbitant; only very wealthy businessmen can indulge this luxury. To "inaugurate" a virgin geisha can cost $2,000 to $4,000.

By Japanese definition, a geisha is the ultimate woman. Like a Japanese garden entirely pieced together by the hand of man, immaculately trimmed, cut, and controlled, she is a work of art, a masterpiece of the aesthetic imagination. She wears sumptuous kimonos; a complete geisha wardrobe can cost up to $3,000. She has the face of a doll, painted white, with a perfectly studied expression.

Always interesting, the conversation of a geisha may range from politics through literature and art. Often she is able to converse in one or two foreign languages. She is capable of telling countless jokes and stories; she dances, sings, and accompanies herself on the *samisen* or the *koto*. All this is quite innocent and pure.

Hostesses are merely caricatures of real geisha, but they have the advantage of being much less costly and more accessible. Every evening, they "take care" of men by the millions. They are the washers and masseuses of the baths, the ladies of the bars, the hostess-waitresses of the restaurants. In restaurants, they serve the client and hand him his chopsticks; they remain close by, ready to light his cigarette, or pour his drink; they keep their clients company and try to amuse them. In bars—there are 80,000 in Tokyo—from the most intimate (one hostess) to the largest (2,000 hostesses in a certain bar in Osaka), they distract the client and fill, for a suspended moment, his fantasies. The hostess is, in turn, confessor, mother, and nurse. The man-child is painstakingly cared for. Be he a president of a company, or a lowly employee, he will finish his evening purring to his makeshift nurse and patting the hand that his indifferent hostess extends as if it were a toy. Except in rare moments of indulgence, for either romantic or mercenary reasons, and for special clients only, it never goes further than this. During long hours every day, thousands of women, queens of the nocturnal nurseries, manipulate men like pawns.

The Revenge of the Sexes

One can say that there are two races in Japan: the masculine and the feminine. The male is irrevocably tied to society. The minute he is hired for his first job, his career is almost irrevocably mapped out. He is prisoner to a conformism he does not think of daring to break.

Women are much more detached. Inferior from birth, totally subjugated and controlled by men, Japanese women are, nonetheless, more free than Japanese men. In her household, the Japanese woman holds the purse strings, a right that tradition reserves for her in exchange for her servitude. During the Occupation, the difficult conditions of life taught her how to economize; her savings were the beginnings of the new Japanese economy. In her home where she is so often left alone by her husband, she has acquired a great moral authority.

The missionaries of the Buddhist sect *Soka Gakkai* did not make a mistake when they decided that the way to convert families to their order was by reaching the women. While Japanese men are paralyzed with the fear of losing a job or a career, the loss of a job is no catastrophe for a Japanese woman. Hence, the women are freer to question the ways of society and business. Three quarters of the divorces (one divorce for every ten marriages a year) are requested by women.

Under the Occupation, MacArthur emancipated women:

He gave them political rights; he opened to them the doors of higher education. Eighty-five out of every hundred public educational institutions are coed. In certain universities, women make up the overwhelming majority. Women have a near monopoly in certain literary and artistic fields, in translating foreign language and in music, for example. Two thirds of the female population belong to some kind of active women's association.

Television has perfected the liberation of women. Household appliances have given her more free time. And despite the supplications of despondent peasant bachelors, young girls are leaving the villages for the big cities.

Under the guise of being submissive, docile creatures, women have often displayed more courage and self-assurance than their husbands. They are more assertive, more open, less furtive. They even possess a sense of humor a rare quality in Japan—and a more confident approach to life. And this is threatening to the Japanese male ego. Durin the 1950's, the novelist Abe founded The Association of Those Who Have a Phobia About Their Wives. A few years ago, a young writer published a book which had quite a bit of success: *How to Re-become a Husband with Authority.* It is because he lacks this authority that the male flees his conjugal domicile and spends his evenings and vacations with his pals, and excludes his wife from his more serious business affairs.

Japanese mythology has always been dominated by women. It was the goddess Izanami who gave birth to the Japanese islands and to the elements of nature. Amaterasu, The August Divinity Who Shines in Heaven, is female. At the dawn of Japanese civilization, women played a key role in the development of artistic and intellectual life. From the 5th to the 12th centuries, life at the imperial court gravitated around women and their intrigues. Japanese literature was born from the pens of Japanese noblewomen; the first great work of Japanese literature, *Genji Monogatari,* was written by a woman. In the 8th century, an empress attempted to break the imperial line by trying to bequeath her throne to her lover, a monk.

But Japanese men had their revenge. The discreditation of women began in the 12th century. Women were accounted to be "subversive" elements. They were excluded from the stages of the theater, where to this day, female roles are still played by men. Confucius held women in contempt because they were "difficult to govern": They disturbed the Spartan existence of the samurai, the asceticism of the monks, and the discipline of the soldiers. They disturbed the perfect control of self so necessary to conformism. Moralizers proclaimed women's defects: "intractibility, bad tempers, jealousy, slanderousness, and stupidity."

Frightened by the charms, as well as by the delicious defects of a real woman, the Japanese male created for his pleasure an image of woman who was as unnatural as she was accommodating: the geisha. Cold and artificial, she is, nevertheless, the perfect woman. Fragile and elusive, she permits men to remain immersed in his fantasy, far from the real world of flesh-and-blood woman, frivolous, unreliable, intuitive woman.

The obsession with unattainable beauty and perfection is typically Japanese. In a novel based on historic fact, *The Golden Pavilion,* by the young Mishima, a monk who stuttered and was singularly ugly sets fire to an architectural masterpiece that was his only passion in life.

The golden pavilion is woman—a superior beauty with whom erotic contact means death. This theme recurs constantly in literature, in the works of Tanizaki and Nobel Prize winner Kawabata.

Impotence and Homosexuality

A degree of physical frailty may play a role in the Japanese man's feeling of inferiority with respect to woman, but there is an even stronger physiological basis for it. Japanese men are sexually less virile than Europeans; serious studies of Japanese sexology confirm this. For Japanese women who have had relations with Europeans, this is an undeniable fact. European women living in Tokyo confide that one Western lover is worth several Japanese. The very hot bath, with temperatures over 90° Fahrenheit, which the Japanese have taken every day for centuries may have something to do with this.

That the problem of virility is grave is attested to by the great popularity of aphrodisiacs. The Japanese use them constantly. The effect of these drugs or powders is much more psychological than physical. In the streets leading to temples and other tourist meccas, displayed amid the other souvenirs, you can find extractions of the most unlikely origins: plants, roots, lizard powders, ground turtle shells, and even bowls of serpent soup. Elixirs of love, and all the famous Japanese sex instruments—musical bells, sheaths, rings, and other accessories—seem more designed to sustain desire than to arouse it. They may even replace desire, as would be the case with the great assortment of phalluses made of wood, either lacquered or covered in tortoise shell, which have been traditional sexual objects of Japanese arts and crafts for ages.

The Japanese woman has, perhaps, some responsibility for this state of affairs. Subjugated as she must be to her husband, she remains a passive partner in lovemaking. But the path from docility to participation takes but a few lessons and a bit of good will.

Voyeurism is a habit that the Japanese learn as children as they peek through the slits in bamboo room dividers. In Japanese prints representing erotic scenes, one often sees a hidden character who is attentively taking in an intimate scene, a child, a servant, a friend. The painter himself by the way he depicts the scene casts himself in the role of voyeur and loves every minute of it. Right up to the outlawing of prostitution in 1958, for which the puritanical pressures of the American occupiers are greatly responsible, an inexpensive side show was available in certain quarters to any curious passers-by. For 100 yen (25¢), a girl would offer a man a match and raise her skirts, under which she was naked. The look lasted until the match burned out.

Voyeurism in its pure state pervades all of Japanese night life: in the photographic studios where the girls pose nude; in the sexy clubs where acrobatic exhibitionism in an area of four square feet lasts two minutes, and is available for an audience of one; or in the roadside stands where the crowds push forward for a peek at sexual intercourse.

One is often surprised at the degree of narcissism the young Japanese display. The lonely and uneasy preoccupation with self, a heritage passed down from the samurai hermits, seems inevitable in a country where the boys are separated most of the time from the girls. In the streets of Tokyo, where the young, "with it" people gather dressed in their tight-fitting clothes, they all seem to be parading in front of a mirror. They seem desperately to be seeking confirmation of their superiority in the fearful and submissive visages of the women.

Homosexuality should not be surprising in a country in which a man has so much difficulty relating spontaneously and intimately to a woman. The prevalence of homosexuality struck Francis Xavier when he debarked in Kyushu in 1549. Homosexuality is not frowned upon in Japan, nor elsewhere in Asia. Before the war, it was a natural part of barracks life, and was even encouraged. In the monasteries of ancient times, and even in the boarding schools of today, it has always been allowed. In the cities, homosexuals have their own clubs and bars, where the hostesses and geishas are transvestites.

In the Japanese theater, the roles of women are always played by men. The male actor of the *kabuki* corresponds to the star of the Follies or the Lido. The famous writer Tanizaki, whose work is marked by his passionate quest for woman, wrote in *The Diary of an Old Fool* that, in his youth, he had one of the most memorable experiences of his life with one of these young actors. Fascinated by the grace of his acting, he invited the young actor to his home. The "femininity" and the "know-how" of the actor yielded, he confessed, a sublime night of love.

Certain Japanese complexes have endowed the sexual influences of the West with special importance. Japanese males are fascinated by white women, but do not have the self-confidence to approach them openly. The platinum blonde is often the main attraction in a *stripou-tisou;* her success is proportionate to the ampleness of her figure.

The secret desire of every Japanese male during one of his trips to the West is an "adventure," or rather, an "experience," with an easy woman of Paris or Hamburg, often coveted for her physical endowment. The Japanese woman allows herself to be easily seduced by a white man—just for the experience, she will say. But often she acquires a taste for this; many girls in Tokyo pursue only foreigners. When the occupying forces left Japan, there were many women on the docks tearfully waving good-by.

A mixed marriage—white and yellow—is very rare in Japan. Mixed liaisons, however, are quite frequent. Many foreign men, both young and old, live in Japan because of their sexual success there. Even the least aggressive and the most homely Caucasian is automatically dubbed a *pure-boy* (playboy). His broad shoulders, his height, his longer nose, his light-colored hair, the hair on his hands and chest—these and a little money willingly spent guarantee an easy victory.

In Japan, an agreeable surprise awaits lovers of night life: Sex is not taboo, nor shameful. Europe, entrenched in 20 centuries of Christianity, associates sex with sin. Christian morality disapproves, a priori, the flesh and its pleasures. In Japan, sex is natural. This can be gathered from the erotic prints and the endless procession of phalluses spread over the Japanese countryside. Sex is treated frankly in daring shows, which a European might call dirty or disgusting. There is no gesture, word, or situation which shocks the Japanese spectator, who is often invited to join in the show.

The Word "Love" Does Not Exist
in Japanese

Among the young, love might be translated as *desire, incli-
nation*, or *making love*. Romantic love is an imported product. The rare young men who, in the streets, hold their
girls round the waist, or stop to neck on a bench do not
seem to be very sure of their methods. In households where
marriages were not made for love, lovemaking is a physiological function.

A Japanese proverb says: "Man marries a woman in
order to borrow her belly." The husband is very jealous of
his child, who is nursed for a long time and kept in his
mother's bed until the age of two or more. Japanese houses
are built in such a way as to make any kind of privacy and
intimacy between parents extremely difficult. In the cities
of Japan, there exist thousands of special little hotels, completely respectable, where married couples, no less respectable, rent rooms by the hour. These hotels come in many
varieties and prices. Most of them are simple, anonymous,
functional—four walls, tatamis, a television set. But some offer more "charm." One, for example, at two dollars an hour,
boasts a heart-shaped bathroom, soft multi-colored lights,
stained-glass windows, a bottle of "love-potion" on a table,
the mirrored haremlike bathroom with gilded transparent
glass partitions, completely equipped with a beribboned
basket containing a contraceptive kit.

Happiness? This word has no meaning for the Japanese.

Furthermore, they look with disdain upon the fanatical Westerners who search vainly all their lives for a state of being everyone realizes does not exist.

The woman is content to dream about romantic love, but even if love remains a dream, she does not consider herself unhappy. If she is in a state of physical well-being, she is satisfied.

This is not true for the Japanese male. Too solicitous of the privacy of others, he cannot meet his own emotional need for close communication; he is very much alone. The incredibly rich and varied night life that is available as an escape hatch does not really satisfy him. It is too sad, too automatic, too sexy to meet real human needs. Communication between human beings, which is essential for both physical and spiritual love, is a universal quest. In Japan, it is pathetically lacking.

Mother Enterprise

At 9:15 A.M., all of the employees have already punched in. On the walls of the cloakroom there is a sign: the 3 S's— SMILE, SPEED, SINCERITY. This is the slogan of one "departo" (department store) of Tokyo. It is in all rooms where personnel congregate: offices, lunchrooms, toilets. There is not one elevator, corridor, or dressing room where the 3 S's cannot be seen. They are driven into the employee's brain.

9:30 A.M. All of the salesgirls are in their uniforms. To soft background music, they go to their counters and prepare their displays. Loudspeakers, on all ten floors, blast forth the morning message of the store's director. Instructions on special items, tips on how to sell more, figures and comments on recent sales, and sometimes a bit of information or news, in order to give the store a connection with the life of the outside world.

9:40 A.M. *Ding!* On every floor the salesgirls form a circle around their superintendent. Greetings and bows are exchanged. The girls are briefed on the work of the day.

9:45 A.M. A record plays energetic, "geometric" music which is piped to all ten floors. It is the daily exercise period. At each counter, the salesgirls go through their warm-up routines, "Rock-your-head, raise-your-arms, on-your-toes, deep-knee-bend, jump-jump-jump!"

Following this exercise, a few syrupy melodies allow for relaxation. And then ready for the Attack!

Ta-ra-ta-ta. At 9:55 A.M. on the dot, a short passage from a classical masterpiece—Beethoven's Ninth Symphony, Dvorak's New World Symphony—barrel out of the loudspeakers—a final, perfect touch to the conditioning of the personnel. All the charming little Pavlovian puppets in miniskirts are now standing in front of their counters, ready to serve their country.

9:58 A.M. The Store Anthem is sung by a philharmonic choir. A double line of hostesses march in step, Indian file, toward the main entrance. The General Manager, himself, conducts the official daily opening. Outside, the first clients wait for the cathedral to open its doors.

10:00 A.M. A bell rings. The hostesses, their faces turned toward the doors, execute, with perfect precision, a collective salute. The manager takes out his keys and, solemn as a beadle, opens the doors. The clients push through the double line of hostesses, who remain in place, bowing and wishing all customers welcome with a pasted-on smile. The loudspeakers bellow "Welcome, honorable clients, welcome to our store. Take your time and enjoy yourselves. Welcome, honorable clients, good morning and welcome."

To really enjoy this spectacle, one must be among the first to enter the *departo.* In the front of the store, at the foot of a gigantic goddess painted on a cathedral window, an organist plays a potpourri of religious music and marches. The procession of consumers begins. From the basement to the top floor, the entire corps of salesgirls stands at attention. All of them bow as you pass. You feel as if you're reviewing troops, and you have an almost overpowering desire to scream, *"Break ranks!"*

Honorable Clients

The Japanese know the secrets of conditioning of clients as well as of employees. Each client is treated like a lord by the white-gloved reception committee. This committee lines the stairs, constantly wiping the bannisters with spanking-clean white cloths. They stand ready, willing, and able to answer questions and give directions.

The elevator operators conduct you upstairs with the sweetest voices and gestures. If you have the slightest question, your salesgirl will immediately call an "expert" who will furnish the necessary answer. The expert, whether in china, paper, or lingerie, knows the answers to everything.

The customer is successively lulled by sweet music and mellifluous shopping advice, and assailed by screeching commercials and hysterical announcements of sales. The client may touch everything he sees, knock over piles of merchandise, upset displays; the salesgirl will never lose her plastic smile.

One department store head even went so far to suggest to his workers that they relinquish their subway seats to anyone carrying the store's shopping bags. The customer need never feel obliged to buy; store personnel have received strict instructions not to discourage or disturb the window-shoppers.

As a matter of fact, the Japanese often go to department stores not to buy, but to relax, to distract themselves, to meet friends. The *departo* offers its customers everything: a choice of 10 or 15 restaurants with every type of food from snacks to gourmet dinners; massage salons; hairdressers; valuable antiques and cheap odds and ends; art galleries and exhibits. On the roof, an outdoor terrace contains a little Shinto sanctuary where one can relax between purchases; a day nursery just like a fair, complete with rides and games and animated story figures; the notorious fishing tank; aquariums; a little zoo of monkeys; red flamingos and penguins; a miniature forest for children homesick for the country; a marionette theater. In order to trap the housewife, the department store has spared neither imagination nor money.

With its atmosphere of country fair and in its social and cultural roles, the *departo* is reminiscent of the temples of the old. Tokyo has over 30 of these consumer sanctuaries, and new ones go up all the time. Sales figures each year zoom to hundreds of millions of dollars. Most *departos* are at least 10 stories high, and close to a city block long. They are often served by private subway lines, with stations opening directly into their basements.

The *departos* also aspire to be cultural centers. In addition to art galleries, they have experimental theaters and cinemas. In fact, to their own advantage, the department stores have become the patrons of the great cultural events in Japan. They sponsor all kinds of artists. Not only have they popularized and vulgarized the culture of Japan, but they have also commercialized the culture of foreign countries. Foreign exhibit weeks are frequent.

To be sure, pains are taken to give authenticity to these events. The Dalai Lama is invited to inaugurate an exhibit of Tibetan art; a South American minister, passing through, will open a special two-week exhibit dedicated to Latin America. But needless to say, the purpose is always commercial. In a Russian exhibit, Lenin exhorts viewers to buy the *departo's* vodka and caviar. During "German week," Beethoven is blared to attract shoppers to the Sony hi-fi merchandise. Imported wines and cheeses represent French culture.

Hitachi and its Counterparts*

Four hundred souls are seated in tight rows in complete silence. The personnel director and his staff enter, in dinner clothes, and take their places behind two tables situated at either end of a platform. The master of ceremonies claps his hands. Everyone stands in unison and bows deeply. *Ohayo gozaimasu.* Good day.

The personnel director replies in kind to this greeting, and climbs to the podium.

"Welcome to the home of Hitachi," he begins. "Our enterprise embodies Japan, but contributes also, by the sale of its products throughout the entire world, to the well-being of all humanity. You know our slogan: DEVOTION, COOPERATION, WORK. Devotion means that each and every one of you should give the best of yourself, and find in your role in our company a meaning to your life. Cooperation means that you should always think and work as a team. Our success does not depend on the value of each of our employees, but on the cohesion of the teams. Do not try to thrust yourself out front; your superiors will

*The description which follows of the concept and organization of a large business enterprise in Japan is based on the author's research into the following enterprises: Hitachi (the biggest organization in Japan. It manufactures just about everything), Matsushita (electronics), Honda (cars and motorcycles), Nissan (cars), the Ministry of Foreign Affairs, the Matsuya department store, and NHK (Japanese radio-television).

discover your qualities by themselves, and give you the credit you deserve.

"Finally, work. In this company, you will not find the easy life of school years, where you were able to sleep during classes and you had frequent vacations. Work is hard. Allow me to give you a few pointers. Do not go to bed too late at night. Avoid going out too often at night to drink, or to play *mah jongg* or to dance. If you are tired, the next day your colleagues will pay for it.

"You are all part of the Hitachi family, a family of 175,000 members. Wherever you go, you can wear our company emblem. Try to remain worthy to represent it."

When the head of personnel has finished his speech of welcome to the new employees, they rise and remain standing perfectly still, looking straight ahead. From the first row, a young man with his head freshly shaved steps forward two steps. He unrolls a long, white scroll, studded with gold, which he holds before him at chin height.

"I thank you in the name of my comrades for this touching welcome and your kind words. We enter Hitachi with great pride and joy. We shall, from this day forth, pledge our lives to company service. We shall work to the best of our ability, and shall try not to disappoint you. We shall try to represent Hitachi with honor, and to contribute to its prosperity."

All assembled now sing the Hitachi hymn:

> *"We will all work to build a better world.*
> *In order to serve Japan and humanity,*
> *We dedicate ourselves to render our com-*
> *pany even stronger.*
> *Workmen, employees, officers, see our*
> *production rise*

> *As the morning star toward the zenith.*
> *Hitachi! Hitachi! Hitachi!"*

Now it is time for photograph taking. Behind the personnel chief and his staff are four rows of stony faces. *Click, click.* The unforgettable day—day of their marriage to Mother Enterprise—is recorded forever. These young recruits enter into the company as into a religion. Until the day of their retirement, they will faithfully carry out the vows they have just made.

The mystery of the extraordinary economic success of Japan is solved. In and of itself, this ceremony of indoctrination almost explains it all.

Most of these employees are between 19 and 24 years of age. Some have recently been churned out from Hitachi training schools, which are to be found in Hitachiville, a town of 100,000 inhabitants and the capital of Japan's industrial empire. From their birth, these workers belonged to the Hitachi family and were destined one day to serve her.

Others have been recruited from the best universities in Japan. They are all very proud of their affiliation. And they have reason to be. Their parents made every sacrifice to put them into the best schools, from first grade through university. They worked like slaves during all their college years in order one day to be eligible for a job in a nationally known, prestigious company. Companies such as Hitachi hire only Japan's young elite. And the elite are often subjected to company "entrance examinations" so that the company guarantees itself the *crème de la crème*. A situation such as that which existed during part of the 1960's in the U.S., where appreciable numbers of the nation's young elite rejected the sham of big business success, would be inconceivable in Japan.

Till Death Do Us Part

If one is so fortunate as to be employed by an important national company in Japan, one never leaves. He is there for life. The conditions and interest of the work are secondary; the only thing that matters is the prestige of the company. When a young Japanese applies for a job, he does not dream of discussing salary. He will be paid according to the pay scale his degrees, training, and age command.

The rare quitter will find great difficulty in getting himself hired by another concern of equal prestige. He will be considered suspect, unreliable, someone in whom it is difficult to have confidence. In fact, he will be stamped with the label of traitor.

Advancement depends almost solely on seniority. Anyone foolish enough to quit one company and join another—even if he managed to pull it off—would have to start at the bottom all over again.

Why, indeed, should one want to leave a job with a good company, where one's future is secure and one's happiness is guaranteed? The employee has the security of belonging to a great family, a modern embodiment of the feudal clan. His membership satisfies his need for group living. In his conversation, he will say "my" company. He will always wear his company button in his buttonhole, even while on vacation. He is very proud of his affiliation and considers himself at all times as a kind of public relations representative for his company. To safeguard his company's reputation, he will watch his behavior carefully, as much during his non-professional moments as during his working hours. When he indulges his need for entertainment, he will present himself to the bar or bath hostess as, first and foremost, an employee of his particular company. His company is his badge of respectability. He will even justify any advances he makes to his hostess by his professional importance. After all, to the gods—that is, those fortunate enough to be employed by his prestigious concern—anything is permitted.

Employees of the same office or workshop consider themselves brothers. Their relationship to their direct superiors is usually excellent—respectful and friendly at the same time. Their superiors are their older brothers. It is a good idea to flatter them and to present them with gifts every now and then, upon returning from vacation, for instance. Hierarchy is revered, never questioned nor ridiculed. A worker bows to his foreman; he in turn bows to his chief, who in turn bows to the director of the division. All of them drop their eyes to the ground before the great president of their company.

A subordinate does not resent the class difference between himself and his superior. The difference in their salaries is slight. An engineer wears the same blue cottons as a workman. Executives and workers share the same offices, often at desks side by side. The only privileged employee is the head of a department who usually has his own office "at the end of the hall." This modest office, encumbered with the same profusion of papers and documents, carries no external status symbol. The executives are never brutal, rarely pull rank on their subordinates. The dignity of all is respected.

Decisions are collective. They are always made after much consultation, even if this takes days and weeks. But once they are made, they are scrupulously and whole-heartedly observed and applied. When one visits the offices of a big company, one is impressed with the number of "rap sessions" going on in corners everywhere, and by the number of conferences in the many rooms reserved expressly for that purpose.

In a word, Japanese workers like their work. According to a national survey, the Nippons feel that their two principal qualities are their devotion to their work and their perseverance. A questionnaire at the Hitachi company produced the following replies: 70 percent asserted that their jobs were the most important single thing in their lives. Many noted, in addition, that their jobs meant more than their wives.

Their ambitions? Most of them aspired to become specialists in their areas of work; some expressed a wish to "outdo rival firms," or to "contribute to the prosperity of humanity"; some proclaimed, "I am proud to think that my machines are in operation throughout the whole world, and thus render permanent homage to my work."

Japanese workers are fanatically devoted to production quotas. In many companies, workers and directors alike sing the company anthem daily at the end of the day. They get together in the evening to discuss the day's accomplishments, to examine their approaches and results, and to debate how to improve work techniques. These attitudes are not far removed from the attitudes in Mao's China. In Japanese workshops, posters read: EACH ONE WORKING FOR ALL MAKES THE JOB EASIER; TO SERVE NISSAN IS TO SERVE THE WHOLE WORLD; WITH I. H. I. FOREVER, WE STRIVE UNCEASINGLY TO PRODUCE MORE. The workers of Hitachi wear an armband labeled ZD, which stands for

Zero Defect. In the waiting room of Matsushita, three slogans are hung on the wall: BE LOVED BY OTHERS; BE SOUND OF BODY AND MIND; and BE RICH AT HEART.

With such psychological conditioning, participation in work becomes an emotional matter. It is not surprising that the Japanese worker has a sense of absolute devotion toward his company.

Nevertheless, he is at the disposal of his employer who is free to transfer him, or to change his job altogether.

Often, in order to give the new recruit flexibility, the novitiate will be assigned to various manual jobs requiring no intellectual capacity. For example, an engineer will put in a few weeks punching holes in tickets at train stations before he is assigned to direct station traffic. His employer will put him through the paces in different departments. It is never certain that a recruit will get the job that his studies prepared him for. A Doctor of Law, hired by a bank, might spend years just counting bills before he finds himself one day as head of the accounting department.

Incubation in the Dormitory

The boss's power is absolute. The state rarely mixes in his affairs; social legislation is limited. But the boss grants his employees benefits which are often well above the legal minimums. He is not despotic. He has all the attitudes of a good family man toward his children. In exchange for the loyalty of his employees, he assures them security and happiness.

First of all, he guarantees them job stability. Firing or laying off employees, just because there is a slowdown in business, is unheard of. An inadequate associate is never let go; he is redirected, with all due deference, to a sideline. An incompetent recruit is treated with all the gentleness one would show a retarded child. A "bad egg" is automatically ostracized by his comrades; the boss doesn't even have to hint at the problem. If a company must get rid of one of its employees—a rare occurrence—it feels duty bound to first find him another job.

Work advancement, except at the executive level, is automatic. Increases in salary follow a carefully scheduled timetable based on degrees and seniority. Trying too hard to excel can compromise a career. Acquiring responsibilities depends more on the "right attitude" than on special talents. The employee who finds a new work method which results in a higher production rate still has to wait his turn for promotion; his immediate superior will draw the benefits of his invention. Modesty and self-abnegation are the primary qualities desired in workers and junior executives. Imaginative, brilliant minds are considered suspect. This concept appears on the surface to be wasteful of talent. But it gives Japanese industry a most effective internal cohesiveness.

Western businesses impute the low prices of Japanese goods to low wages. At first glance, Japanese salaries are noticeably lower than their Western counterparts. This might suggest an exploitative system, and the spare Japanese starting salaries confirm this impression. A high school graduate will start work with a salary of between $50 to $90 a month; a college graduate starts at somewhere between $70 and $120 a month, his salary being, at this stage, less than that of his subordinates. During the first years of employment, however, advancement is very fast. This system pacifies the workers and makes for stability in employment. In 1970, the average wage in Japan for thirty million salaried workers was around $160 a month. The difference in salary between workers and executives is far less than in the West.

But the monthly salary represents only a half or two thirds of the total income. To the salary must be added other considerable benefits. These benefits give the employee of a big Japanese company almost the same income as his European—if not his U.S.—counterpart. Two times a year, in June and in December, every Japanese worker gets a bonus which adds to his annual salary, three to seven months' wages—up to twelve months at Honda. Now that the bonus has become an institution, it is at once a gesture of generosity on the part of the employer, a reward for production, and profit-sharing tactic. This system of deferred payments in effect forces the employee to save money; meanwhile the system keeps the substantial accumulation of interest on the money in the company till.

The workers do not seem to notice or care about this. No union in Japan has challenged this system. The semi-annual distribution of bonuses delights the banks; 30 million salaried workers, forced into frugality, deposit two thirds of their bonus in one shot. Of the seven billion dollars distributed in bonuses in 1969, more than four billion were deposited in savings accounts. (These fabulous savings help explain Japan's spectacular investment rate.)

More than two billion dollars were paid out by big business in Japan on expense accounts in 1969. Expense accounts are another kind of indirect salary, a salary that is free of taxes. White collar workers are the main beneficiaries. For an executive in the middle brackets, his expense account may mean as much as $500 or $600 extra every month. A worker who earns as little as $100 a month might spend several hundred dollars in one single night entertaining clients.

Expense accounts attest to the prestige of a firm. They help to keep a million bar and club hostesses employed and support several hundred geisha. (It is thus not surprising that one must pay exorbitant fees to enjoy a luxurious night life in Japan.)

In lieu of a general system of social security, the big company will furnish its employees gratis with its own social security setup. The big company employs a corps of dentists and doctors, has its own specialists and its own hospitals. Often the company allows an extra pension for each child, and also provides accident and life insurance.

When he reaches retirement age (55, except for executives), the employee has a choice of accepting a monthly pension or a lump sum as severance pay. The lump sum is the more popular choice. This sum represents something between 40 and 50 months of salary—about $20,000 for an average retired person who has spent 30 years with a company. For the senior executives, of course, these figures run much higher.

There are still other sundry bonuses and fringe benefits given for excellence of performance, transportation expenses, or to one who has put in an unusual amount of overtime. Some Japanese companies provide low-cut cost or no-cost loans to an employee who may want to purchase a house or a car. Some companies also provide free transportation. Others run company canteens, cooperative shopping centers.

For executives, companies pay for membership in a golf club—an indispensable but very costly status symbol for the Japanese businessman. Senior executives may be provided with chauffeured cars at company expense. These benefits are bestowed both to reinforce the paternalistic life style, and to enhance the image of the company.

A boss must also be concerned with housing his personnel. So entire neighborhoods of low-cost housing, ranging from apartments to cottages, are constructed near the company's factories. Dormitories are placed at the disposal of single men and single women. Though these very often look like army barracks, and their comfort factor is minimal, they are practically given to the employee free of charge. Though the dormitories are sex segregated, the bathrooms are communal. Heating is often non-existent. In the girls' dormitory, curfew is between 10:00 and 11:00—no later. Visits from members of the opposite sex are not allowed; such socializing would have an ill effect on productivity and on the reputation of the house. Young workers usually like their dormitories. "All of the people I work with are friends, and after work, we get together and continue to discuss our ways of working and living," explained a young worker to me.

Vacation Camps for Adults

Japanese paternalism borders on maternalism. Not only does it concern itself with workers' security and comfort, but also with their physical, cultural, and spiritual well-being.

Private baseball and football fields, tennis courts, and sometimes golf ranges, pools, gymnasiums, judo rings, d'aikido, and boxing rings—all are available. The employees have their choice.

The company also constructs and runs free sports clubs for its employees. Collective sports are particularly encouraged, because they extend team spirit. Sports enthusiasts are given every opportunity to keep in training, and to organize teams for competitions. Those who excel are even given time off from work for sports endeavors. If they become champions, they benefit from quicker promotions.

Most of Japan's great sportsmen, in fact, work for the big national companies. The champion baseball team works at the national newspaper *Yomiuri*. The majority of women volleyball medalists at the recent Mexican Olympics are employees of one of the many Hitachi factories of Japan.

Japanese efficiency experts are canny: Gymnastics before and during work periods improve production. Such gymnastics are the rule in almost all the big Japanese outfits.

Exercise equipment is everywhere. From your hotel room in Tokyo, you can take your field glasses, focus on the terrace of any industrial building within range, and you will see Japan doing its calisthenics. A bell rings. Executives and employees alike, white and blue collar, climb to the workout roofs of their buildings and take their positions. A loudspeaker hoarsely plays music by Chopin or Schumann, and everyone jumps, bends, turns, bobs, stretches, and swings arms—all in perfect unison.

The boss also provides libraries, discotheques, and movie clubs for the cultural nourishment of his workers. In some companies, girls can take free courses in flower arrangement "so that their personal refinement and artistic taste which will reflect in their work" (specifies the Seiko watch manufacturer). Some companies publish their own daily or weekly bulletins; some put out a whole magazine filled with news of the company's glorious achievements and those of its loyal workers.

Hitachi is not the only company which has its own training school. The technical institutes run by private companies are usually of a very high quality and very up-to-date. They often include day care centers where working mothers can leave their infants.

Many companies give Saturday afternoon off, in addition to the usual Sunday off. The two-day weekend is beginning to become more widespread. In addition, there are 12 other paid holidays during the year. The legal minimum number of holidays a company must allow its workers is six days. The big companies generally give two or three weeks. But no one would dare take all these holidays, much less all at one time. Vacation days not taken are often paid at double time. In any case, vacations never go beyond a few days, or a week at the most. The right thing to do is not to take more than a few days off at a time. This is a tremendous advantage to business, and to the economy in general, since there is not the usual holiday slowdown.

The company, of course, sees that its personnel and

their families get sufficient relaxation. Workers and dependents are offered free excursions. On such excursions, the sexes are separated, but this does not disturb the male workers one whit. It is tacitly understood that one does not refuse to participate in these annual outings.

Workers can spend their personal vacations at an adult vacation colony, and send their children to a live-in camp. (Honda has constructed a Disneyland for the children of its personnel at the Suzuka factory.) Or a worker can choose to vacation at one of the hotel chains, or at the thermal cure station, or a sea or mountain resort—all of which are exclusively reserved for company employees. Costs are minimal. One company even constructed a hotel exclusively for the use of company honeymoon couples!

Here is a sample of a release distributed to the Tokyo press: "The employees of Nissan Motor Company have taken, for the third time in the history of the company, a week's vacation that they say they enjoyed immensely. It must be remembered that Nissan was the first in Japan to institute a general week's holiday. This formula has impressed the public as being ingenious. Most of the employees were thrilled with their week of camping at the youth festival. The members of the Nissan baseball team got enough training to be able to carry off trophies in the next intercity tournament. Now the workers of Nissan are hale and hearty, having lived under a strict regimen prescribed by our health experts. They can now once more devote their energies to the production of cars of international rank."

Many firms also find it advantageous to provide collective recreation from time to time during the working day. This enhances the team spirit. On the slightest pretext, a foreman will at the end of the day gather his workers around one of the machines or at a desk and serve bottles of beer, sake, and snacks. Everyone will toast the prosperity of the company. On these occasions, one must drink up; abstinence is frowned upon. Or, the foreman will invite the men out for a little tour of the clubs—at company expense, of course. In February and March, restaurants and bars make their biggest profits of the year; this is the time when whatever money is left over in a section budget has to be used up before the end of the fiscal period, which begins April 1st in Japan. Naturally, the most luxurious clubs and bars are chosen for these crash sprees.

A number of times during the year, a company celebration will have all the workers congregate around the big boss. Fun and laughter as well as speeches are in order. All the accessories for festivity are distributed at the door: confetti, firecrackers, whistles, crepe throwers, etc. And when the big boss gives the signal, all begin to laugh and fool around. "You can kid the boss tonight; it's okay."

Someone looks as though he has problems, seems unhappy. His superior will observe him for awhile, and will then invite him out to dinner. Very tactfully, but insistently, the superior will try to find out what the problem is. Romance? Money? Family affairs? There is nothing like getting it off your chest to your superior. "Everything will work out, you'll see."

If a worker becomes nervous, Mr. Matsushita, of the Matsushita company, has invented an infallible therapeutic technique. The patient is taken into a room where the walls are made of deforming mirrors. If the patient does not laugh, it means his case is serious. He then has to go on to the next room. An effigy of Mr. Matsushita hangs from the ceiling and with a sign: TAKE HOLD OF THIS IDIOT, HIT HIM, PUNCH HIM HARD. After the patient has been relieved of his aggressions, he is taken through still another door to lie down on an analyst's couch. A tape recorder begins. The voice of Mr. Matsushita himself unwinds, comforting and strong. The boss lectures soothingly on morals and tells the way to happiness through the Matsushita Electric Company.

The kindness of the managerial staff even invades the private life of the employee. Just about every company celebrates the marriage of a worker, or the birth of a child. Companies run dating services for the single, and marriage counseling services for the married. The head of a department or chief of a section will always attend the marriage of one of his men; the president does the same for his executives. Honda offers free furniture to newlyweds. If the father of one of the employees is ill and dying, the son will receive a plane ticket to go to see him, no matter how far off he may live. Some firms assume the funeral expenses of a loyal employee. From the cradle to the grave, millions of workers live under the protective wings of Mother Enterprise.

This concept of company life, or rather this technique for greater production—since that is what it really is—this stupefying psychological integration of the worker, this systematic paternalism is chosen, not imposed. A national poll conducted by the newspaper *Mainichi* proved that conclusively. The question was: "Between a superior who does not push you to work any more than the rules require, but who does not take interest in you outside of working hours, and a superior who makes you work hard but takes care of you outside of working hours, which do you prefer?" Eighty-five percent preferred the latter.

Unionism, Operetta-Style

It is meeting day for the company union. Every employee, without exception, wears a large plastic company armband. At a given hour, all the machines stop. Everyone gets up and goes toward the corridors. Calmly seated in their chairs, the section managers, assistant managers, and supervisors watch them leave, much the way teachers smilingly watch children go out to play at recess. I asked one of these pontiffs if he ever went on strike. He looked at me with disbelief for a moment and then in condescension to my ignorance, deigned to answer. "Never. I am a boss, and bosses do not go on strike."

About 50 people are now assembled in front of the elevator. One of the union men shouts into a microphone, an unnecessary gimmick in such close quarters. Each worker has a funereal expression on his face. The subject at hand is a demand for a 19 percent increase in salary, rather than the 13 percent proposed by management. The nerve! "Last year, management gave us 15 percent. The enormous investments our company is now making . . . the evaluation of profits . . . the increase in capital . . . how can they justify offering. . . ." A motion of protest is adopted unanimously. There are two minutes of silence, in order to complete the 20 minutes allotted for the strike meeting. Then everyone goes back to his post, silently and swiftly.

In the big companies, where the employees consider

themselves lucky with their lot, where the relationships between worker and management are excellent, where the
employee is kept informed and is regularly consulted, where
the notion of a class struggle does not exist, how can the
unions play anything but a marginal role? The workers
themselves consider their relationship with management to
be more important than their relationship with the union.

First of all, the unions themselves are part of the company. Their directors have to be approved by the management. At times, management even defines the union's duties.
I know one company where the president himself heads the
union. Of course, all the workers, without exception (except
the junior and senior executives) are affiliated. The union
meeting halls are furnished by the company. To simplify
things, union dues are taken directly out of salaries by the
company.

One third of the workers in Japan belong to company
unions, which are not organized either horizontally into
crafts or vertically by industry. Outside of these company
unions, there are four large unions, of which the most important is the Sohyo, whose membership, now numbering
three million, has been declining in recent years. Government employees constitute its chief membership. Participation in unions in small companies is minimal. And among
the several millions of temporary and dayworkers, there
are no unions at all.

Since social problems are solved at the company level
—not the national level—these paper tiger unions never become actively involved in social conflicts.

With little else to do, they throw themselves into sterile
political action such as protesting American bases on Japanese soil, or advocating the rearmament of Japan, which
only causes disaffection in the ranks.

They also pay lip service to the class war; but class

struggle is a concept the ordinary Japanese worker cannot, by and large, understand. He doesn't think of questioning the structure of his company, much less of society as a whole.

On the whole, the unions support, rather than undermine the paternalism of industry. They are mainly concerned with salaries. Union and management representatives discuss their problems over a cup of tea; often they know in advance that they will easily reach a compromise. For appearances, to prove that they serve some purpose, the union will call a strike for the benefit of the employees—with the full consent of management. These ritualistic walkouts are very short-lived and are usually planned months in advance, allowing ample time to arrange for no loss in production; but needless to say, they take place much less often than in Western countries. Nationwide general strikes are practically impossible in Japan, a situation that gives Japan a considerable economic advantage.

Mr. Honda in the Canteen

For many workers in Western countries, the big boss is an elusive enemy, safely enshrined in his tower of gold. Not for the Japanese worker. A Japanese company president is totally involved, day by day, with his employees and their work. Mr. Honda, for example, whose name embellishes one out of three motorcycles used throughout the world, spends most of his time in his workshops, dressed in blue cottons. His hands dripping with oil, he leans over a motor. He takes his meals in the canteen. To the workers he frequently sees, he is almost a pal. His assistants keep him completely informed of even the most insignificant problems that affect his workers.

A boss in Japan wouldn't think of making major decisions alone, or only with his chief, without consulting his subordinates. For example, in 1969 the president of a large bank (Daï Schi Bank) announced his intention of merging with another large bank (Mitsubishi Bank.) However, the negotiations had to be suspended because of severe criticism from executives who had not been consulted. Subsequently, the president was forced to resign.

A Japanese company president proposes much more than he imposes; projects are suggested to him, rather than initiated by him. Every project, as it goes through the hierarchy, can be profoundly modified or altogether changed. At each level, a project receives due consideration by section leaders who are careful not to seem too arrogant about suggesting modifications that might interfere with the general consensus. In its collective approach, Japanese enterprise is much more democratic than big business in the West.

A company president in Japan delegates a maximum of authority. His role is that of arbiter. One big difference between him and his Western counterpart is that he lives a calm life; he has time to think about his relationships. His office is not a panic area. His desk is orderly: a pad of paper, a few newspapers, several files, one or two telephones. He is not disturbed except for important matters.

With the maximum of his energy oriented toward his work, his personal life is simple, his standard of living modest. Ostentation would shock his employees; in any case, it would not correspond to his personal tastes and instincts. His residence is not luxurious, no Rolls Royce, no yacht, no vacations in the Bahamas, no expensive socializing. If he does spend large sums of money on geisha, good restaurants, golf, or around-the-world-trips, it is usually done on an expense account, and for professional reasons.

For example, Mr. Komai, the president of Hitachi, a small man with a quiet, timid countenance, lives in the suburbs in a simple house surrounded by a small garden. He takes a commuter train to work; and he spends his rare leisure hours playing golf, reading, and painting in watercolors.

The Japanese executive is, in fact, not necessarily rich. But he is sincere when he says: "Even if I were rich, I would live as simply." The Japanese executive, by and large, is a salaried worker, not the proprietor of the business. Mr. Honda is a rare exception. The *zaibatsu* (the rich classes) which existed before the war were broken up during the Occupation; they have been restored but their capital has been disseminated. Mr. Komai, for example, holds only a fractional percentage of the total shares of Hitachi, most of which are spread through banks, insurance companies, real estate firms, and the like.

Capitalism in Japan is of a very special variety; the collective good takes precedence over personal gain. This is true for both workers and bosses. As for shareholders, management wouldn't think of distributing to them extremely large dividends; the increase in the nominal value of their holdings suffices.

The Sacred College

Fountains everywhere, and fifteen stories of glass and steel, with Gothic touches. Inside, one encounters mahogany, marble, and rich, thick carpets. The Keidanren, the supreme court of the Japanese businessman, is an ultra modern cathedral in the center of Tokyo. It is from here that the high priests of Japanese industry orchestrate the economic and political destiny of the country.

Without doubt, the Keidanren is the most powerful organization in Japan. The power behind the throne, it is for its members, at once the judge, the jury, the promoter, the executor, and the controller. The presidents of the biggest businesses and industries gather here to determine levels of productions, salary scales, investments, mergers. Bent over a map of the world, they weigh the pros and cons of the exploitation of the sea's natural resources, the ramifications of activities in Africa, exploring the riches of Siberia or Indonesia, the opening of new trade barriers, and the nature of the commercial attack to be perpetrated on Europe. Special committees concentrate on foreign trade, commercial navigation, transportation, education, finance, armament, international relations. The Keidanren absolutely controls the country.

It is before the Keidanren's special committees that government ministers propose reforms and suggest experiments. It is this or that committee director who pushes the country into expanding the aeronautics industry. Without the go-ahead of the Keidanren, the government cannot decide to rearm the country, to increase aid to other Asian countries, to recognize or not to recognize mainland China. This brain trust participates in every important national decision, and this extraordinary system assures that every political decision will be taken with full consideration of its impact on business.

The almost perfect cohesion that exists among the members of this club of business giants is a natural extension of the excellent relationships which exist inside the individual companies. The Keidanren forms a community of interests unique in the world. Business magnates and bank tycoons cooperate smoothly to control competition and to realize more profits. The common denominator is the best interests of the nation. That prime concern produces the sacrifices and solidarity which prevail. Herein, in yet another form, lies the secret of the great strength of the Japanese economy.

If two companies get into a tug of war and begin competing in a way which might damage the whole industry, their competitors will get together and act as mediators until the matter is settled. If foreign competitors begin to threaten, Japanese companies get together to reduce costs. If there is a danger of overproduction in one sector, as was the case with the steel industry a few years ago, everyone will get together and limit investments. If one company is in danger because of a drop in its production rate, the banks will "make a collection" to help it modernize and stay in the running.

This community of interests is quite natural when one realizes that the directors of all these various companies and industries came from the same universities and from the same social background. The "elders" of the big universities of Japan form indestructible clans. More than one third of the presidents and director-generals of the big companies have graduated from Tokyo University. And nearly two thirds of these directors attended one of just three of the other 687 universities of Japan.

Nepotism plays an important role. Personal relationships and family relationships are paramount. A survey showed that one third of the sons of the presidents and executive directors of large firms go to work for the companies with which their fathers are affiliated. A survey among lower echelons would undoubtedly have yielded the same results; sons of workers also tend to follow in their fathers' footsteps.

Homogeneity of management is reinforced by the existence of the *Zaibatsu,* which through its four enormous industrial and banking empires (Mitsubishi, Mitsui, Sumitomo, and Fuji) controls a third of the affairs of the country.

However, the greatest determinant of unity is the inalterable interdependence between banks and industry. The high-powered economic growth of post-war Japan depended as much on the solidarity between these groups as on their individual progress. The continuing boom of the Japanese economy during the last 20 years is due to the most impressive re-investment effort: one third of the total national product each year. Compare this to one fifth in Europe, and one sixth in the U.S. Loans were, and still are, the chief means of financing expansion. In 1968, the debts of the 500 most important Japanese firms represented about 3.5 times their own funds. As for their capital ratio, their total assets were no more than 20 percent or 30 percent (in the West the ratios are the reverse).

Banks make loans freely, and are not subject to legal restrictions. Many banks virtually do not have a yen in their vaults. They juggle funds by borrowing money themselves, from day to day, in order to maintain a running treasury. In disbelief, Western observers cry *Catastrophe!* but the system has always worked, and it appears, will go on working. This has been going on since the Occupation. When the American banker Horace Dodge was given the task of straightening out the monetary chaos of post war Japan, he declared that the state budget must always be balanced, a principle which may have appeared stupid at the time. Mr. Dodge rendered a great service to Japan. Immense sums were necessary to reconstruct the factories. Since they couldn't count on the government, manufacturers went to the banks, and the reconstruction of Japan was accomplished entirely on credit. One dozen Japanese banks control the market for capital in Japan.

Ever since then, the big guns of finance and the captains of industry have been obliged to pedal the same tandem in order to remain upright. In constant debt, the manufacturers must expand, in order to be able to pay their loans; while the banks are condemned to continually extend their loans in order to make expansion possible. With one hand, the banker hands out money; with the other, he draws in interest on capital and dividends on preferred shares—which is limited by law to 10 percent—he holds. With one eye on its own books of account, and the other on those of its debtors, a bank commonly delegates one of its own executives, usually a man about to be retired, as a "consultant" to the borrowing firm. The consultant may sit on the board of directors of the indebted company, and will serve the cause of surveillance.

Savings are extraordinarily high in Japan; 20 percent of family income is deposited in banks. But this is not enough revenue. Banks borrow from other banks, or share loans among themselves, the way insurance companies share risk factors. Banks also operate like their clients—they borrow: on the international market, from the bank of Japan, which has often been too generous and required bailing out by American banks; and directly from American banks. In this way, Americans have, in fact, financed the industrial expansion of a country which today, is their biggest competitor in many areas of industry.

Thus in Japan, businessmen, banks, and the Ministry of Finance form a perfect triangle. This unorthodox marriage of interests, composed of orthodox partners (to borrow a phrase from the *Economist*), is certainly the most surprisingly successful working arrangement in the history of contemporary economics.

Business and Politics

In a very comprehensive way, Japanese industrialists offer the Japanese government a perfect synthesis of ideas. The dialogue is effective; the government is not the enemy but the counselor, the natural ally. The government is always kept informed, is always invited to give advice. Business managers gladly permit the ministers of finance and industry to look into their affairs and comment.

Often, a man can go from a high government position to that of a senior executive in private business without even feeling that he's changed careers. These switches are encouraged; they reinforce ties all around. In 1968, 136 high government officials were authorized by the government to move to jobs in private industry; the government saw in this transfer nothing but advantage. Retirement age in the government is 55; most men at that age are still spry and sharp enough to conduct business. Many government specialists moonlight, in a strictly legitimate way, as business counselors; this gives them a foot in the door as against the day they are compelled to retire from government service.

High-ranking bureaucrats are treated by big business like pashas: They are invited to the best restaurants; they are invited for golf weekends; they receive sumptuous presents; they are lent cars with chauffeurs; they are provided with geisha. Sometimes government officials can dine without paying in sumptuous restaurants, and a big firm will pick up the bill. This form of corruption, rarely on a hard cash level, is considered normal. At times, a scandal will cause the exposure of one tenth of the iceberg, but such slips are quickly forgotten.

In fact, often officials involved in scandals are nevertheless reelected. Mr. Arafune, involved in the infamous black mist of corruption in 1966, was dismissed from his post as minister of transportation for having created a stop in an obscure village in his district for the national express railroad line. He is today vice-president of the lower House. Prime Minister Sato, himself, was implicated in a resounding scandal in 1954 when he was secretary general of the Conservative party. He owes his political life to the unprecedented intervention of the Ministry of Justice.

If a government official, working with a firm as a counselor, reveals a talent for politics, that private business might finance his campaign and start him on a political career. This is an accredited way to become a minister in Japan. Public service is the seeding field for politics. Most of the present ministers, including Prime Minister Eisaku Sato, as well as many deputies, are ex-bureaucrats.

Big business brings to power and maintains in power those who know how to take care of its interests. Business spends considerable sums to keep the conservative party in power. Inside the party, big business wheels and deals with the factions which support big business. Mr. Sato wholeheartedly supports big business. He has been Prime Minister for eight years—a record. During the general elections in December, 1969, big business poured more than 30 million dollars into Sato's electoral campaign. In Japan, political investments always pay off. Mr. Sato walked off with an impressive victory, and assured his party a healthy majority. He controls 300 deputies out of 486.

It would be inconceivable in Japan for a party and a

prime minister to gain power if they were opposed by business, although from time to time business extends small favors to opposition parties and to the large unions. (One must maintain favor everywhere . . . one never knows.) The great weakness of the parties on the left is explained in part by their meager finances. Only the Komeito party, the political arm of the powerful Soka Gakkai sect, has money that compares with that of the Conservative party.

"Never So Few Men . . ."

Business has thus had at its disposal, through its control of politicians, technocrats who represent the best needs of the country.

Assisted by computers, the Japanese technocrats of finance and industry are the craftsmen of the best-planned economic system existing today. They are constantly producing long, medium, and short-term auxiliary programs that are interdependent, yet mesh together beautifully.

For any project undertaken, there are always guidelines. The Japanese accumulate masses of statistics based on yearly, monthly, weekly, daily, even hourly surveys covering the entire economy of every industry. They make detailed studies of their own production techniques, and analyze the production problems and successes of other countries.

Japan is always working on a five-year plan; it is a goal which is taken seriously, always realized, and often surpassed. Without any protest from the unions, the government systematically directs its energies toward those sectors that are most important for the prosperity of the country, neglecting those sectors that are less vital economically. Competent government technocrats decide which industries should merge, what research should be undertaken, fiscal and export-import procedures. They do this with every confidence that they are working for the national interest. In serene intimacy and solidarity, an oligarchy of bankers, businessmen, and technocrats direct the destiny of the country. "Never have so few men done so much for their country." Churchill's words referring to the airmen who rescued England from the German Air Force, are equally applicable to the men who run the Japanese economy.

How would one characterize the economic system of Japan? Is it Capitalistic? Socialistic? Communistic? Well, it's a little of each.

It is not completely capitalistic, despite the violently competitive spirit of its industries. Not when businessmen must consult each other and the government before concluding deals with foreign firms. It is not socialistic, despite the tight scale of salaries, and the merciless, progressively rising rate of taxes—much higher than what prevails in Europe or in the U.S.A. But no socialist country keeps public services to a strict minimum. One never talks of nationalizing the utilities or even all the transportation. Nor is it communistic, despite the great measure of collectivism in industry. It is inconceivable that the means of production could be in any but private hands. Nor does the notion of class struggle exist. The Japanese economy has not been government-owned since the Meiji era when the state gave an elitist impetus to economic expansion by developing factories, which it then sold for next to nothing to Japan's privileged families.

A few catch phrases for describing Japan's present economy come to mind: *Paternalistic Economy, Modified Planned Economy, Modern Feudalism, Industrial Oligarchy*. Let us say that the Japanese economic system is collectivist capitalism, which tends to become capitalistic collectivism.

Japan is often compared to a gigantic ant colony in which each member, by virtue of his birth and his education, accomplishes the job which is assigned to him. Or one could compare the country to a beehive, in which all the bees nourish one Queen. In no other country, is there a similar concentration of energies: first, at the service of the Emperor; then, at the service of an illusory military power, and now at the service of economic growth.

The Exploitation of Small Business

Employees, executives, presidents, captains of industry, and government executives form a compact pyramid, at the top of which floats the banner of ultranationalistic progress. But this pyramid rests upon a base of an invisible, suffering, silent segment of the country's economic fabric. Japan's salaried workers are powerless observers of the profit and progress merry-go-round.

The majority of Japan's workers are employed by small businesses, firms which are desperately hanging onto their crumbs of profit and are almost totally at the mercy of the huge corporate giants. The majority of these businesses just manage to survive. Their employees have no weekend or vacation benefits, and no social security, their tiny bonuses and small salaries amount to half of those earned by workers of comparable level employed by the big companies. The standard of living of the majority of these workers is hardly glittering.

One is stunned by the cheap prices of Japanese cars and Japanese boats. These prices are made possible by endless, small, sub-contractor workshops, all of which are dirty, badly equipped, and hidden at the ends of dead-end streets in slums and suburbs, yet situated, to be sure, within a few miles of the big production lines. These small companies must sell at the lowest possible price, offer the best service, and display constant deference and respect, in the way of flattery and gifts, to the big companies who allow them to live. If the larger companies stopped their orders, the small companies would perish. The smallest recession, however camouflaged, can mean instant bankruptcy to many thousands of these remnants of the 19th century. If hit by a recession a big business can live for a time on its income from its stocks and bonds, or it may be able to stall its creditors. A small business has no such safety valves, and therefore it is extremely easy for a big business to blackmail these powerless underlings.

For these poor cousins, life has become more and more precarious. The small nondescript firms constitute the expendable refuse of Japan's prosperity boom. They are prey to competitors with cheap, sub-quality products made in Korea, or in Formosa, or in Hong Kong. Small businesses are the first victims of price increases and cost of living increases. They can never find banks willing to extend them credit; banks and the government loan only to the rich.

But small businessmen and their employees are not at the very bottom of the heap. Temporary or dayworkers rank even lower. These unfortunates are at the mercy of recruiting gangsters for port or building construction firms; they are the workers who build those superb highways which encompass Tokyo above and below ground, who work without rest periods in every kind of weather, day and night. It goes without saying that they are even more poorly paid than the workers in small business. No one protects their human rights, let alone their pay rates. Nor do they know how to defend themselves; they are the uneducated, disinherited peasants from the villages.

There are also the million and a half laborers who work in their own homes, and who, in order to buy their daily ration of rice, accept from their "protectors" the kind of contracts which guarantee a life of poverty.

Japan, then, mercilessly sacrifices to her prosperity the aged, the educationally and physically handicapped, the weak. According to a survey conducted by Japan's Ministry of Health in 1969, only one 65-year-old man out of five was receiving a pension. In order to live, 83 percent of those over 60 depend on their children. Two thirds of the country's old men, and one quarter of her old women, must continue to work to stay alive. Outside of big industry, there is no social security, no retirement pensions, no guaranteed housing, little comfort, and less hope.

Powerhouse of Progress

In 1968, Westerners who went to the Olympic games in Tokyo viewed at close range the extent of Japan's postwar reconstruction. That's when the talk about the "Japanese economic miracle" started. But once the games were over, Japan was forgotten. Japan went its unobtrusive way, and left the headlines behind. The Sony transistors, the Honda motorcycles, the Nikon cameras, the fleets of tankers—they reminded the West every now and then of the existence, on the other side of the world, of the land of the gadgets and the cheap production costs.

Then, in 1968, Japan celebrated the Meiji centenary, the culmination of a hundred years of effort that catapulted the country into modern times. And world experts began to analyze the mechanisms of Japan's extraordinary development. At the futuristic exposition in Osaka, a world's fair more Japanese than international, the experts began to ask THE question: Exactly where does the Japanese powerhouse plan to go?

"Banzai! Banzai! Banzai!"

Once upon a time, back in the year 1969, the fairy tale begins, they gathered in the court of the statisticians of Japan, adding and re-adding the long columns of figures. They couldn't believe their eyes: In 1968, the Japanese gross national product amounted to 142 billion dollars.

All the gentlemen took off their glasses and looked at each other. Was not that the figure set as a goal for 1971? There must be an error somewhere.

And then each went back to his drawing board, started from scratch, consulted his computers. A few days later, the figures came out again: In 1968, the Japanese gross national product was a stunning, a colossal, an incredible 142 billion dollars. *Banzai! Banzai! Banzai!*

But the victory cry did not last long. In a typically Japanese reaction, each statistician ran into his own office: The figures must be compared to those of the great white powers. The figures rolled out: Italy: 71.5 billion dollars. France: 127 billion dollars. U.S.S.R.: 350 billion dollars. U.S.A.: 860 billion dollars. West Germany: 132 billion dollars. There were more banzais all around; Japan had passed West Germany, and had become the third economic power of the world.

That evening, in public restaurants and private households everyone celebrated. They drank to the eternal prosperity of the nation and to the health of their leaders. Europe had been overtaken; the next step was to catch up with Russia.

During the next few days there was a statistical festival in the economic ministries. All sorts of calculations were made. From 10 billion dollars in 1950 to 200 billion dollars in 1970 meant that the GNP had, in 20 years, multiplied by 20. In 10 years, industrial production had quadrupled; in many branches—metallurgy, chemistry, and petroleum, for instance—production had quintupled. In other industries, productivity had multiplied by 6, or by 10, and by even more. Another interesting figure noted along the way was that the rates of increase in salaries in Japan had always remained far below the increase in production. In any case, there was no longer any need for the Japanese to feel inferior to the Europeans. Their per capita income had approached, and would soon surpass, that of the major European countries. The Japanese were on their way to becoming rich—very rich.

Soon the celebrations were over, and one and all went back to their calculations. What would they do next? Where would they set their goals? But now goals would be set for an even longer range. Directors set their men to work getting detailed sets of figures. Even small business had reason to rejoice and be proud of the results. Let us look at what the figures showed.

For about 20 key industrial products, Japan ranks as the second or third producer in the world. Its production represents almost half of American production, about 50 percent more than German production, and as much as the combined production of France and Great Britain. Production per person is equal or superior in all sectors [except woolen fibers] to that achieved in the European Common Market.

Here is how Japan's industrial production compared

with the combined production of the six countries of the Common Market in 1968: electricity: 50%; cement and cotton thread: 50%; cars, steel and aluminum, sulfuric acid, plastics and resins, paper cartons: two thirds; synthetic fibers: 90%; televisions: 130%; copper: seven times the production of the Common Market. By 1970 all these rates were even higher, since Japan's production increased more rapidly than that of Europe.

For the last dozen years, one ship out of every two constructed in the world has been Japanese. Naval construction in Japan has doubled since 1962. In 1969, the 350 Japanese shipyards christened 9 million tons of ships. Two thirds of these were for export. These shipyards, by the way, employed only 120,000 people, a very small work force for such huge production.

More than half of the motorcycles produced in the world are Japanese—around 4 million in 1969. Mr. Honda alone manufactured 2 million. One of his factories in Suzuka, near Nagoya, was completely built and in operation within seven months, from cutting down the trees on the land to the emergence of the first unit on the assembly line. Here, a motorcycle is produced every eight seconds. In 1966, when his motors ran away with all prizes in all categories, Mr. Honda installed branches in every corner of the world. Without any doubt, Honda and Sony have done more to enhance the Japanese reputation abroad than all their industrial colleagues put together.

One out of every two photographers in the world—both amateur and professional—uses a Japanese camera. The quality of these cameras, not to speak of their low cost, is unbeatable. Asahi Pentax was the first firm to launch the photographic reflex system. Nikon lenses compare well with those of German Leicas.

Japan is first, by far, in the production of sewing machines. It produces half the machines in the world.

And Japan leads the world in the sale of transistor radios, pianos, organs, and electronic microscopes.

The Japanese are also the best fishermen in the world; and produce more rice per square foot of cultivated paddy than any other country.

In many areas, Japanese industry is second in rank in the production of automobiles, in general electronics, in petrochemicals. In plastics and resins, synthetic rubber, artificial fibers, cotton and wool fibers, clocks and optical goods, refined copper, zinc, aluminum, newsprint, bicycles, games, beer—the increase has been formidable.

In 1960, the Japanese auto industry produced only 500,000 cars a year; most of these were light trucks or other functional vehicles. After 1966, the auto industry took off. In two years, it had doubled the production figures of Italy, England, France, and West Germany.

The Europeans, still ahead in the production of pleasure cars, were stupefied. Then, in 1970, Japanese pleasure car production reached close to 5 million. In four years— from 1967 to 1970—Japan's private-car production doubled. Toyota and Nissan, with 1,750,000 and 1,500,000 cars respectively, rate as the fifth and sixth car manufacturers of the world. The best-known Japanese car manufacturer in Europe, Honda, who, in 1966, branched into automobiles for exportation, is only the third largest car manufacturer in Japan.

The Japanese are small; they like small things, and they know how to make small things; they are masters of electronic miniaturization. Noting the numerous Japanese who wear large eyeglasses on their small noses, Robert Guillian wrote that, "they are able to put a propitious myopia to great advantage in minute operations." Some of their radios, which weigh but a few ounces, are no bigger than a matchbox;

their TV bracelets seem to come out of science fiction. They produce small things on a big scale, and are by far the best in the field.

Japan's electronics industry has an extraordinary vitality. In this area, Japan's skilled technicians are the most original and inventive in the world: In 1958, they came up with the first diode semiconductor; in 1961, a series of transistor magnetophones for television; more recently, with new diodes, color television, electronic microscopes. The Japanese are the world's second largest producers of TV sets—6½ million sets in 1969.

The electronics industry, where Mr. Matsushita is king, seems capable of producing an infinite variety of products to meet limitless needs. His plants manufacture electrical gadgets for the kitchen, hi-fi sets, color TV, and air conditioners as well as electrical apparatus for industry.

Today, his factories are going full speed ahead with computers.

Japan is the third largest producer in the world of heavy electrical equipment, chemical products, glass, paper, cement, and steel. In steel, Japan is the world's third largest producer, but if growth continues on the present scale by 1975 Japan will probably be first, ahead of the U.S. in steel production. Japanese production of steel is equal to the total combined production of Germany, Great Britain, and France. Its steel industry is the most modern in the world, with the largest furnaces.

Japan provides two thirds of all petroleum the world requires. She is the third largest producer of electric power. Her own consumption of energy equals one third of that of all of the six nations of the Common Market put together.

The Third Biggest Business

Industrial power leads to commercial power. The volume of Japanese exports has been steadily rising, and reached over fifteen billion dollars in 1970, making Japan the third largest exporter after the United States and Germany.

Ever since 1968, Japan has exported much more than she has imported. In 1970, the national money reserve was over four billion dollars. Almost the entire Japanese cash reserve is in dollars, which explains her tendency to align with Washington on sticky questions concerning international currencies. Japan is no longer a country in debt running from one international bank to another to get credit in U.S. or Eurodollars. The yen has become, along with the German mark, one of the two hardest currencies in the world. Not one day goes by where the press does not mention something about the inevitable re-evaluation of the yen. When the control of exchange rates is lifted, the yen will certainly become one of the strongest international currencies.

Since 1970, Japan's huge merchant fleet ranks second in the world. It is ahead of Great Britain, just after Liberia. Japan will soon boast the leading merchant marine in the world. Also worthy of note is the fact that Japan Air Lines has extended its banner, as of 1969, over a network of almost 160,000 miles, making it the eighth biggest airline in the world.

Transformed in 1949 and patterned after the methods of Wall Street, Japan's stock-market exchange has multiplied its volume by 380 since the war, a record rate. Today, Tokyo is, after Wall Street, the second greatest financial center of the world.

One Boat out of Two

Let us visit one of these industries in which Japan has made not only astonishing increases in production, but remarkable innovations as well. The shipbuilding industry is a good example.

Japanese ships are constructed faster and cheaper than any others in the world. The method is practically 100 percent assembly line. The selection of steel plates and sections is automatic.

In a dark room, a photo enlargement projector prints the lines and curves of a blueprint on steel plates, on sections treated with special powder. An automatic blowtorch cuts along the lines and curves. As these pieces advance along the assembly line, they are put together by giant soldering machines, each weighing several tons. Enormous cranes then place the assembled sections together until the hull is formed. The rest of the ship is then structured as though it were made of giant building blocks. This operation requires 500 workers and technicians. The duration of the operation is four months for the body, and four months more for the installation of small parts equipment. Eight months later almost to the day, the finished ship is loaded with its first cargo of petroleum, and sent on its way, for instance, to the Persian Gulf. Scarcely has this mastodon taken to the sea than the keel is being laid for the next ship.

For once, it is the Europeans who copy the Japanese.

Europe now has about 20 Japanese-type shipyards; and these receive more construction orders than their prototypes. In the face of this kind of disturbing competition, the Japanese have started studies on a new type of cargo vessel, which is atomically propelled.

Son of an Ironsmith

There is probably no other country in the world in which workers have as many positive qualities as the Japanese. The Japanese worker is the social mechanism par excellence, an almost perfect instrument. He is an indefatigable worker, loyal, devoted to the last. He is the strength of the country.

Japanese workers are united in their decision to win the world economic race by the year 2000. Everything having to do with the economy of Japan is considered by each citizen to be of personal interest. In this respect, popular capitalism prevails. (One Japanese out of four possesses an investment portfolio, compared to one Frenchman out of twenty-two.)

Japan has its legion of "self-made men"; men who started with nothing and built vast industrial or commercial empires, such as Sony and Honda. In 1947, Mr. Ibuka founded Sony with a capital of 500 dollars and seven employees, whom he called the seven samurai. Today, he has multiplied his capital 4 million times. He only has 10,000 employees, but boasts, in addition, 1,000 doctors of science who devote themselves to research. Their inventions rival those of General Electric.

Japan's capitalism has its quota of Horatio Alger stories. Mr. Honda, who is "Pop" to his employees—not Mr. President—is the son of an ironsmith. After the war, with parts he got from American surpluses, he built his first motorbikes piecemeal. Since he had no gas or carburetor fuel of any kind, he used an extract drawn from roots. Today, he mass produces "everything that has a motor, that roars and smells of oil." "Don't talk to me of electric motors," is his favorite saying.

In 1918, Mr. Matsushita, son of a poor peasant, was a young electrician with two employees in his service. Today, he employs 50,000 workers, spread throughout the 50 branches of his business. He owes his initial amazing success to the electric rice cooker he invented shortly after the war. Thanks to him, millions of wives can get up half an hour later every morning. Mr. Matsushita sells an incredibly varied line of electric gadgets and appliances on credit.

Mr. Toyoko owned a small piece of land not far from the center of Tokyo. On it, he constructed a cinema house—on credit, of course. To attract more people to his theater, he built his own subway line to reach it. To keep his patrons coming, he constructed a whole neighborhood of boutiques and cafés. Soon thereafter, he embellished the whole area with a department store. He is thus responsible for the creation of the liveliest section of Tokyo, the well known Shibuya quarter.

In 1952, Mr. Shoriki, the president of *Yomiuri*, the popular daily newspaper (daily circulation: 9 million) got the revolutionary idea of creating a commercial television network. To launch his idea, he brought a few hundred sets from the U.S. and set these up on street corners in Tokyo. He didn't have a yen in his pocket and his journalists were even asked to forego their salaries for a period. It did not take long for commercial TV to make Mr. Shoriki a very rich man.

Permanent Education

The leaders of this prodigious economy are educated, informed, energetic, and young.

In 1868, feudal Japan was already one of the most literate countries of the world. Today, one worker out of five has a high school diploma, a ratio surpassed only in the United States. With 99.9 percent of Japanese children attending school for nine years, Japan enjoys the highest rate of literacy in the world. Eighty percent pursue a secondary education, and 20 percent eventually attend a university. Many adults devote their leisure time to perfecting their skills or to learning foreign languages, often under the auspices of educational television. The application of students to their studies—both young and old alike—never ceases to impress.

Fifty million copies of daily newspapers circulate in Japan (as against 15 million in France); and 20 or 30 million copies of weeklies, monthlies, and specialized publications. There are 78 private radio and television companies.

In Japan, there is a radio and at least one TV set in every home. The educational and cultural channel, NHK, operates from dawn to midnight.

The dissemination of information is monumental. In the dailies, 50 percent of the space is devoted to political, economic, technical, and cultural affairs; in the more serious papers these matters occupy three fourths of the space. The largest paper, the *Asahi*, circulates 10 million copies; the *Yomiuri* 9 million, and the *Mainichi* 8 million. The economic press prints 3 million copies daily; more than half of them being editions of the *Nihon Keizai*, which no major or minor official would ever miss. A children's publication, the *Yoehen*, prints 700,000 copies. A survey showed that an introductory course in data processing on television was followed by 700,000 persons.

In 1969, there were more than 15 million telephones in Japan, with more than 2 million additional phones slated for installation in 1970. The telephone in Japan works perfectly; and the cost of using phones is half of what it is in France. However, not every household has a phone; business has priority and phone booths are everywhere—in front of restaurants, bakeries, pharmacies.

Some more examples of the energy and mobility of the Japanese: Travelers within the country log over 150 billion passenger miles a year on railroads. This is another world record. National tourism is practically a civic duty.

The *Tokaido* bullet train between Tokyo and Osaka (over 300 miles; a three-hour journey at about 125 miles per hour) transports over 200,000 passengers each day.

The Japanese have set records as well for the construction of highways and for maritime coastal trade.

The country's swift economic growth is explained to some extent by the youth of the population. One out of two Japanese is less than 26 years old. After the war, the baby boom further pressured the economic acceleration; whatever the cost, the country had to create jobs for a million new job hunters every year. The youthfulness of the working population explains, in part, why the average salary is low; novices receive very low salaries. The size of the working force is more and more linked to the economic strength of the country. Out of 103 million inhabitants in 1970, there were 50 million workers, and 85 percent of these were employed in industry and services, a very high proportion indeed.

This youthful vitality is also reflected in sports. At the Olympics in Mexico, the little Japanese were third in collecting medals. In May, 1970, a Japanese expedition conquered Everest. At the same time, lower down at an altitude of 2,500 feet, Yuchiro Miura was shussing, at over 90 miles an hour, down two miles of virgin mountains on the "roof of Asia."

Does the spiritual life of Japan show the same resilence? We shall see that it vacillates.

Thanks to the War

Man, the essential motor force in the economic boom, benefited from a lucky set of circumstances and from natural gifts, apparently unfavorable but eventually very propitious. The social essayist, Oya, writes:

> The difference between the industrial power of Japan and that of Great Britain since the War is due to the difference between the destructive ability of the B-29 and the destructive ability of the Messerschmitt.
>
> The German planes did little more than scratch the British factories, which after the War were put back into their pre-War—and already outdated—working shape. With us, the American super-fortresses razed everything to the ground; we had to rebuild the whole country from point zero. The defeat of 1945, with its annihilation of our industries, the loss of our colonies—which cost much more than they brought in—and the psychological sting of the American occupation, were all lucky breaks for Japan.

After the war, like Germany, Japan had to start from scratch, profiting, of course, from the manna from America.

For her reconstruction, Japan received from the U.S. more than 2 billion dollars, to which sum one must add all the money the occupiers, transformed into allies by the 1951 San Francisco peace treaty, spent in the country during the occupation. In 1966, for example, these military expenses amounted to 6 million dollars. Moreover, the umbrella of American protection relieved Japan of making any military expenditures. This in itself was an enormous advantage when one realizes that today Japan's military budget is still less than 1 percent of its gross national product (compared to 5 percent in France).

The outbreak of the Korean War in the 1950's couldn't have come at a better time. Japanese industry filled all American military needs and got its first real postwar boost. In 1956, the closing of the Suez Canal galvanized the naval construction and metallurgy industry. After Japan's recession of 1962, the Vietnam conflict came to the rescue. Japanese workers were employed to sew uniforms and make boots for American GI's, while the Japanese chemical industry manufactured explosives. Each step that Lyndon Johnson took toward escalating the war meant one more boost for Japan's stock market. During the last few years, America's involvement in Indochina has yielded Japan orders amounting to a billion dollars a year.

From the skies above, the god Izanagi hurled her lance to the earth below, which was covered with water. When he withdrew his lance, a drop of water dripped off and flowed, creating the island of Onogorojima. To this island Izanagi invited Izanami. And it was from the love of these two that the Japanese islands were born.

The long string of islands brought forth by this divine couple was not very prepossessing: small, tortuous, hunchbacked, with pockmarked coasts, feeble resources. But these infirmities were the saving grace of modern Japan.

Averaging little more than ninety miles across throughout its length, the Japanese archipelago is one third smaller than France (230,000 square miles, compared with 340,-000). Japan's population is, nevertheless, twice that of France (103 million inhabitants, as against 50 million). Only a sixth of Japan's land is arable. This land, intensively cultivated, yields subsistence for all, with no problems of surpluses. Agriculture is, in fact, less heavily subsidized in Japan than in the West. The concentration of population in coastal areas favors the development of industry.

Without a drop of oil of its own, without coal, iron, minerals, Japan has to import 80 percent of its raw materials. This is, actually, an advantage. Japan does not have to try to maintain uneconomical coal and iron mines, as does Europe. Japan buys all its oil, coal, minerals, cotton, and wool wherever it wants, and at the best prices. Transporting it is not very expensive. Bringing a ton of coal across the Pacific is actually less difficult than transporting it by rail from the Ruhr to the steelworks in Lorraine.

There is not a thing for sale in the whole world—iron, copper, phosphates, lead, zinc, or nickel—that the Japanese do not appear as instant purchasers. They debark in the poor countries of Asia, Africa, and South America with large smiles and with magnificent plans for projects, preferably run with their own equipment and technicians. They offer long-term contracts at practically no cost to the country involved. "You will see, there will be much money. And with our yen, you can buy our machines, our beautiful Sony transistors, our shiny Honda motorcycles. We will give you good prices and good credit terms."

Japanese developers have been particularly interested in the kaleidoscopic mineral deposits of Indonesia. And Japan has opened its doors to the great continent of Australia. Today, Japan is Australia's best customer, even surpassing Great Britain. It is a mutually agreeable relationship. Japan appreciates Australia's political stability. In 1965, the two countries signed a fantastic 15-year contract for the sale of 100 million tons of iron minerals. More recently, Japan signed similar contracts for coal with both Australia and Canada. Iron and coke from America, Canada, Chili, Peru, Brazil, India, Malaysia, Mauritania, and Morocco all together are not sufficient for the insatiable appetites of their steel mills.

Even the Russians have invited the Nippons to exploit Siberia for its petroleum, gas, and copper. But the Japanese distrust their powerful neighbor, who is too demanding, both financially and politically.

Japan is the largest importer of petroleum in the world —170 million tons in 1970. Ninety percent of her needs are met by American and British oil wells. Worried about the possible financial and strategic consequences of such dependence, Japan has sought to diversify its sources of supply and has looked to Rumania, Venezuela, Indonesia, and especially Alaska. But Japan would like to produce its own petroleum. Mitsubishi has begun to drill at the bottom of the sea in Japan.

All the raw materials imported by Japan arrive via the least expensive route, the ocean. The materials are dumped directly into the refineries, which, of course, are conveniently located along the coastline.

Japan lives on the sea. Its four large islands, with deep coastal waters and involuted shore lines, provide about 17,000 miles of coastline, twice as much as England for the same surface. What a boon for a modern economy! Lacking space, the Japanese have taken afloat the soil that was missing to them. They weeded hills and threw them into the water, creating artificial islands and banks which could be devoted to industry. These were cheaper to build than artificial land. Japan's technique of drainage is superior to that of the Dutch at Zuider Zee. The space nibbled out by this process is considerable; they anticipate 22,500,000 acres from now until 1985. Little by little, the bay of Tokyo is being filled in on all sides. The white-scarred hills of Kobe watch the sea recede. Everywhere, around the ports of Osaka, Takamatsu, Fukuoka, factories plant their feet in the water. Most of the ultramodern industrial complexes are girded on two or three sides by quays and receive their replenishments of raw materials directly from the cargo holds.

Financial Acrobatics

The mechanism of the Japanese economy is based on one vital necessity: exports. Export or die. Any deficit in the balance of payments would constitute asphyxiation. Japan makes her clothes, TV sets, cars, and most of her homes with imported raw materials. To pay for these materials, Japan must transform them into elaborate products, and sell them to foreign countries, come what may. This requires the most aggressive selling techniques.

Japanese industry has often been accused of dishonest tactics; of benefiting from a government policy which subsidizes exports of all kinds; of lowering prices; and especially of dumping. It is true, that in the past, the Japanese were past masters of the art of dumping. This persists for certain products, such as textiles, cars, and television sets, which are sold at heavy losses in order to capture the markets. Australians are particularly irate about Japanese cars. However, today there are many original products, cheap but of high quality (electronic and photographic equipment), that do away with this practice.

In fact, the Japanese rely more and more on the quality of their products. That is why for the last 20 years the Japanese have continued to invest at a dizzying rate: On the average, a third of the gross Japanese national product is reinvested every year. Compare this with a reinvestment figure of 25 percent in Germany, 20 percent in

France, and 16 percent in the United States.

The Japanese investor often invests for reasons of prestige. He is much less obsessed by concern with immediate returns than his Western counterpart. In the long run, such an attitude pays off.

These investments must achieve quick success because the interest rates on industrial loans run high—anywhere from 8 to 10 percent. The financing of these investments is enough to give any Swiss banker a nightmare. While in the O.C.D.E. countries an investment is usually composed of two thirds capital investment by the entrepreneur, and one third a loan from banks, in Japan the proportions are reversed. European bankers and industrialists who visit Japan get dizzy when they learn that this excessive indebtedness often rests on short-term credit.

This tandem of business and banking has never toppled its virtually forward flight. In the cycle of overindebtedness, overinvestment, and overproduction, Japan has never fallen because the syndrome moves so fast. In case of difficulty, the government effectively intervenes with credit; and the United States can always be counted on to come to the rescue with back-up credit.

All these financial acrobatics are possible because of the Japanese penchant for saving. The Nippons save 20 percent of their profit, as compared with a saving of 9 percent in France, 6 percent in the U.S.A., and 5 percent in England. Personal savings represent 30 percent of national savings—an enormously high proportion. The sense of frugality is traditional.

The biannual distribution of bonuses also helps explain the high rate of saving. And the absence of a general system of social security is another aiding factor; still another is the policy of distributing retirement capital in one lump sum; finally, the high cost of a university education obliges parents to save from the moment a child is born.

Such investment effort is not possible except in a concentrated economy. Heavy industry and chemicals represent two thirds of Japanese industrial production. In *Fortune* Magazine's listings, in 1968, of the 200 largest non-American enterprises in the world, 45 were Japanese, 47 British, 28 German, 21 French. Five companies carrying the name Mitsubishi were on this list.

After the Japanese capitulation which ended World War II, one of MacArthur's first actions was to dismantle the *zaibatsu*, the monopolistic oligarchy of great families which ran and controlled Japanese industry. Their fortunes were confiscated, their financial and industrial tentacles cut and strewn in different directions.

During the Korean War and the recovery of Japan's independence, the *zaibatsu* reinstated themselves; however, this time they were under the control of technocrats who were commoners. Today, directors of various firms belonging to the same *zaibatsu* often run into each other at board meetings, meet more or less officially at conferences, at lunches and at dinners. They renew old ties through loans. Today, their solidarity is basically financially inspired; their bank holding is the catalyst. There are in Japan 12 large city banks. A 1968 survey showed that of the 200 largest banks in the world, classified according to deposits, 30 were Japanese. Four of these Japanese banks had deposits of over 4 billion dollars.

Except for a few independent industrial empires, such as Hitachi, Matsushita, Yawata-Fuji, Japan is not really a country of giant enterprises. The *zaibatsu* seem to be colossi with feet of clay. Mitsui, for example, manufacturer of atomic piles, is active in various industrial territories, but does not hold even one firmly in hand. The branches of these trusts are not as strong as one would think. On the long-postponed eve of the opening of their frontiers to foreign capital, the managers of these trusts were very much aware of this.

For the last few years, in naval construction, metallurgy, and other industries, the country has been going through a frenzy of regrouping or merger, a process largely orchestrated by the banks. In 1967, there were 12 firms in the automobile industry; in 1970, there were seven. Seven are still too many; and regrouping and merger around the two giants, Toyota and Nissan, are in process.

In metallurgy, the merger of Yawata and Fuji puts the new enterprise, with its production of 25 million tons of steel (almost equal to that of all of France) in second place as the world's largest steel producer, behind U.S. Steel, which in 1943 produced 36 million tons.

The government is solidly behind such industrial reorganization. The government easily lends its aid to those who can think big. The case of ethylene is typical. Its production was insufficient so the government launched a development plan. Too many candidates presented themselves. The government set 300,000 tons as the minimum of production per unit, and granted loans only to those units who were capable of fulfilling this quota.

The same concentration applies in commerce. Among more than 6,000 firms, one dozen account for three fourths of Japan's foreign trade, the largest part of this being handled by the three largest *zaibatsu*—Mitsubishi, Mitsui, and Sumimoto.

Mitsubishi Shoji is the biggest commercial enterprise in the world; in 1968 it did over 7 billion dollars worth of business. Whatever is produced must be sold. These specialists in commerce make detailed studies of the markets and offer their services and research findings to industry, even sometimes suggesting new products. They play a very important role in informing not only their suppliers, but also the government, of conditions on all five continents. The selling techniques of European industrialists seem backward by comparison.

Economic Chauvinism

Competition is the spur to economic growth, and competition is particularly acute among the big companies. If one of them should go into the production of a new product, another will follow—sometimes if only for reasons of prestige. New articles, new machines, new outside markets—all these provoke investment spirals.

The spirit of competition exists even between branches of the same company, and between departments within one company. In Matsushita, for example, it is never considered that the losses in one department are balanced out by the gains in another.

There is no mercy for the weak. Small and medium-sized companies are condemned to succeed or die. Every month a great many of them are forced into bankruptcy.

The government contributes a modest, discreet, neutral budget to the free play of the economic market. In 1970, this sum was 25 billion dollars. The increase in government spending has always been less than the increase in national product. Private investments are twice as large as public investments. It is mainly the private sector that provides for housing, research, and a good part of education. Government subsidies are lighter than in European countries and pertain mostly to coal, national transportation, and to agriculture, where the government supports a moderate surplus production of rice. On the whole, governmental expenditures for social welfare are very modest.

Fiscal policy in Japan is much tougher on individual revenue than on corporate revenue. *Productive* investments are always spared from heavy taxation. In fact, the Japanese would consider the heavy taxing of industrial profit and gross income downright immoral.

But Japan does have very high protective tariffs. In this regard, Japan resembles 19th-century England: a great commercial power, and at the same time, a nation closed to foreign products and foreign investments. Japan has turned a deaf ear to the indignant protestations of Europeans and even to those of her greatest partner in commerce, the U.S., with whom she is carrying on a veritable war of nerves. Despite demonstrations in the U.S. against Japanese products, despite agreements, such as those of the "Kennedy Round" which she violates with impunity, Japan hides behind her duty barriers and protects her own industries with unmatched chauvinism.

Fearing foreign capital, the Toyota Motor Corporation amended its statutes to prohibit any foreigner from serving on its advisory board. Japanese industrialists are afraid that foreign investors would introduce a germ into their country that would destroy the paternalism of Japanese enterprise.

Since the war, Japan has been determined to control the exchange. This has become less and less justifiable in view of the important Japanese reserves (over 4 billion dollars in 1970). This policy seems destined to disappear in a few years.

Japan is practically Machiavellian in its efforts to protect its products and its capital. With more than one hundred taxable products, Japan holds the record for the countries of the GATT (General Agreement on Tariffs and

Trade). Its customs taxes are much higher than those of other countries. There are all kinds of laws to discourage competition from foreigners.

This situation is flagrant in the cause of the automobile. Cars imported into Japan are taxed up to one third of their value. In addition to duty, there are various other taxes and endless inspections. However, products which do not compete with domestic products can waltz into Japan with none of this red tape. And when the importation of certain articles can stimulate modernization in certain industries, barriers are lowered.

The Ministry of Agriculture is particularly relentless on the subject of imports. Using as justification the low level of productivity (which is not exactly true), and the inferior quality of Japanese agricultural products (which is true), the ministry allows almost nothing to enter the country. Oh, yes, recently, the ministry made an exception and opened the door to two American products: chewing gum and pâté for cats.

The Japanese government is extremely reluctant to liberalize rules governing foreign investment, and finds all kinds of ways to delay the inevitable moment when foreign investors will be allowed to move into all of Japanese industry. Today, foreign investment is allowed 100 percent in these few industries which do not fear the invasion of foreign capital, such as electronics. In an industry where the danger is minimal, foreign investments are authorized up to 50 percent. But in the majority of cases, foreign capital is 100 percent prohibited.

The government does appreciate joint ventures in industries where the Japanese still have something to learn.

The penetration of foreign capital into the economic paradise of Japan is exceptionally feeble: 700 million dollars in 1969 (mostly American). From 1950 to 1966, American investments in Japan amounted to 200 million dollars; whereas in the six-year period from 1961 to 1966, the amount for France was 735 million dollars, for Germany 1,400 million, and for Great Britain 1,800 million. Thus, Japanese industry has preserved its independence, and raised the American deficit. Enterprises funded wholly by American capital are very few, the major one being the petroleum industry.

Intoxicated with Buying

Surely, pessimists say, the accelerated growth rate of Japan is destined for catastrophe. But, today, this disastrous prognosis does not hold up.

The first potential danger, prognosticators anticipate, could come from a decline in international trade. If, in a world crisis, Japan stopped being a huge exporter, she might rapidly fall to pieces. However, given her gross national product, her percentage of exports is much lower than that of Europe: 10 percent for the Japanese, against 11 percent in France, 15 percent in Great Britain, 18 percent in West Germany, and 34 percent in the Benelux countries.

Here's one example: While the big automobile firms in Europe export half or more of their total production, the two big automobile firms of Japan export only 15 percent of theirs. In case of a world crisis, the Japanese would not suffer more, but rather less than the others.

Another source of possible danger: the increase in social security expenses. But the social security costs in Japan are already almost as high in the large enterprises as they are in Europe. As for salary increases, they are on the upswing—12 percent to 15 percent a year during the last few years. But up to now, the increase in productivity has exceeded the increase in salaries.

Some people predict that Japan will simply overproduce.

Until now, there has not been the slightest sign of this possibility. After the United States, 103 million Japanese form the greatest society of consumers in the world. They are not only producers, as they were during the 1950's; they have become, during the 60's, consummate buyers, as well. In the last five years, their spending has tripled.

In the present society of abundance, being rich is no longer vulgar; the young people want things, and the older generation is, too, sloughing off its traditional frugality. An aggressive advertising campaign has created new needs. Commercialism overruns the streets with neon, caps the roofs of buildings with enormous billboards, sprawls across newspapers, invades television where programs are interrupted by commercials every five or seven minutes or by flashing ads at the bottom of the screen.

Manufacturers of dishwashers put a million machines on the market, in one swoop, in their first year of production. The female market is strenuously pursued. To sell their electrical kitchen equipment, Hitachi formed a women's club. Toshiba offers free cooking courses across the length and breadth of the country.

Most Japanese today possess a television set, a refrigerator, and a washing machine; most every Japanese will possess a color-television set, an air-conditioner, and a car. These items are two to three times cheaper in Japan than they are in Europe. In 1970, the Japanese used close to 5 million color-television sets—twenty times as many as the French.

Soon new status symbols will be called for, probably in the realm of housing, since most Japanese still live in modest houses in neighborhoods enlivened by typically Asiatic disorder. Housing, food, clothing—all are in a process of change. The sales prospects are all the greater since the rate of replacement of old things is extremely high.

And in addition to the domestic market, several hundred million inhabitants of Asia and the Middle East will eventually become clients. And later on, the most fabulous market of all will open—China. Eight hundred million Chinese will naturally look to Japan as their closest and most important supplier.

Paradoxically, in a country as overpopulated as Japan, not one day passes without the daily press alluding to the question of full employment and the grave dangers of inflation which would follow in its wake. A reserve working force will be available for a long time to come. In the rural areas, which still constitute over 20 percent of the population, the birth rate has not dropped. In the underdeveloped industries and in the small cottage industries, unskilled workers are over-abundant. Also, married women usually stop working after the birth of their first child. Then there are the unlikely legions of orderlies, hostesses, wrappers.

And there is much developing in the techniques of automation. There is always a shortage of specialized and skilled workers, but industry has not waited for government action; it trains its own technicians.

What might result in a real slowing-down of economic growth are the national projects which the government is going to have to fund. Highways and roads are insufficient; bigger and better sewage systems are required in almost all of the big cities; new housing is sorely needed; hospital, welfare, and retirement systems scream for increased funds.

There are, in addition, rising governmental expenditures for such things as aid to the third world, rearmament, and building prestige—the Osaka Exposition cost close to 3 billion dollars, and the 1972 Olympics at Sapporo two or three times as much as those in Grenoble, France, in 1968. However, such expenditures would ultimately be of great benefit to the Japanese economy.

Everything except Moon Rocks

The chip in the armor, if there is one, is research. After the Meiji, Japan set itself to systematically copying the West. This permitted a more rapid and less costly growth. But in the long run, a lack of independent research and scientific imagination could be harmful.

Japan's technological dependence on outsiders is still considerable, especially with respect to machinery and chemicals. The large Japanese firms are also more or less tied to foreign companies through technical agreements. Of course, the Japanese always select the very best in each specialty.

The imbalance in scientific exchange is sizable: one patent exported for every ten purchased from abroad. In 1968, Japan devoted 1.8 percent of its national revenue to research, compared with 2 percent in Europe, and 3.8 percent in the United States. Public expenditures are minimal, since the government relies on the diligent efforts of the private sector. If basic research is neglected, it would be to the great disadvantage to Japan's technological future—especially when she gets ready to try her own wings.

However, it must be noted that Japan does not just slavishly or thoughtlessly copy its betters. What comes in from abroad is carefully studied, evaluated, tested with "a thousand sauces" in the laboratory. In fact, it would be rare if the new product were not improved.

In 1968, Japan had 350,000 researchers, which is more than Germany and Great Britain together. Many firms have begun to appreciate the importance of research, and now include in their budgets both men and money for this purpose. Honda employs more than 1,000 doctors of science; Mitsushita, 1,500; Hitachi, 2,000; Toyo Kyogo (Mazda cars with rotary piston motors, a system borrowed and improved from Wenkel) doesn't hire men until they have completed their college degrees.

In certain areas, Japan could give lessons, notably in electronics and metallurgy. Considering the importance attached by the Japanese to a university education, it would seem that in the very near future, Japanese technology will catch up with, if not overtake, the West. This could be a possibility in the fields of space, aeronautics, atomic power, and computers.

At Expo '70 in Osaka, the objects which seemed to have impressed Japanese visitors the most were not the exhibits showing the world of the future, (which seemed to attract most foreign visitors), but the moon rocks exhibited in the American pavilion. Space is still one of the rare domains unknown to the Japanese.

However, in February of 1970, Japan became the fourth country in the world to enter the race into space. After more than four years of futile attempts, the scientists of Tokyo University were successful in placing into space *Osumi*, a small device which was able to send out signals for just a few hours. This Lambda rocket—10 tons, 50 feet, 4 stages—was a homemade automatic guidance system, launched more or less blindly.

But the Japanese putterers of Todaï, who amused themselves launching crude rockets that looked like billiard sticks, are not to be taken lightly just because they got off to a late start. They hold the record for producing the cheapest satellite in the world. And their space program labored under a comparatively tiny budget.

Nor did they benefit from any great popular interest. Displaying a rare slackness, the Japanese government has not yet wholeheartedly decided to propel itself into the space race. Its science department was five years late in initiating its own research with the brains of Todaï. Their modest efforts would, if all proceeds according to plan, permit Japan to launch two dozen experimental scientific satellites by 1975. But Japan must continue in strict cooperation with the United States in its space program.

Japan seems to have decided to close up its aeronautical gap. The Japanese aeronautical industry, dismantled by MacArthur, is still dwarf sized. It produces the notable YS11, a medium carrier with Rolls-Royce turbo-reactors, and the MU-2, a small business plane. The government and the *zaibatsu* do not wish to stop there. Their engineers are laying plans for commercial jets and for military planes. It is almost certain that after having built the Phantom under American license, aviation in Japan will turn purely Japanese in the 1980's.

The bombs which fell on Hiroshima and Nagasaki infested the Japanese with a nuclear allergy, which accounts for their late start in the area of peaceful atomic research. Only in 1966, after a dozen or so years of procrastination, did Japanese industry admit that they were using a maximum of hydro-electric power in a country which cannot draw on any natural resources of coal or petroleum. It was high time, industry admitted, to get seriously interested in atomic energy. It ordered generating stations from the United States. By 1977, 20 reactors will be in operation in Japan—and 38 more will be in construction. In 1985, with 40 million KWH, Japan will have become the second largest producer of nuclear energy in the world.

Today, Japanese companies have contracts with American firms such as General Electric and Westinghouse. But in the future, Japan would like to cut its ties with the American nuclear monopoly and approach a country like France, particularly with regard to the production of the new self-generating super-reactor.

The Japanese atomic industry is directing its efforts in four directions: (1) the creation of a plant for the diffusion of the enriching gases of uranium; (2) producing uranium ore; (3) the recycling of radiated combustibles; (4) the construction of a giant cyclotron.

In 1972, Japan will send afloat her first atomic cargo ship—an entirely domestic product. Yes, Japan intends to catch up fast. When a country plans to become the superpower of the world, the area of nuclear development is much too vital to ignore.

Let me emphasize that today's research is directed entirely toward peaceful ends. But to bridge the gap between the peaceful atom and the military atom, it takes nothing more than one evil thought. Japanese atomic scientists already know how to produce plutonium by reprocessing used uranium. Technically, they could easily put together, by themselves, their own bomb.

Several years ago, the government could not publish any statistics at all—not about births, nor about deaths, nor about marriages. Then it received a computer from the United States from which the Japanese expected miracles to emanate. But the Japanese didn't even know how to use it.

That epoch is gone. Today, the Japanese industry is still behind in the software department, but is actually on a par with European industry in the hardware department. In Europe, three fourths of the computers are installed by

IBM, whereas in Japan computers are built by Japanese firms. Research proceeds apace, and is heavily supported by the government. Fujitsu has manufactured a huge computer strictly on its own. Three major manufacturers have joined forces to produce the software. Growing today at a rate of 27 percent per annum, production will have sextupled from 1966 to 1975.

Computers are in widespread use today—one can reserve tickets on the Tokaido railway, or on Japan Air Lines; or one can get a quick count on the deposits of the main banks. The computer has become the magical instrument, the right arm of big business. In no other country, except the United States, has the computer been used so systematically. It is the symbol of the future.

Watch out for the Nippons!

"The 21st century will belong to Japan. The Japanese will have the highest standard of living in the world," wrote Herman Kahn of New York's Hudson Institute in his 1966 book *The Year 2000*.

This statement was greeted with skepticism by everyone, including the Japanese themselves. Professor Kahn's pronouncement was considered sensational and extravagant. But in 1968, when Japan became the third economic power of the world, beating Professor Kahn's projected schedule by seven years, the skeptics took another look. They consulted their slide rules and computers and came to the conclusion that Professor Kahn's predictions had been too modest.

The Japanese government, itself, couldn't and wouldn't believe it. "This will only stir up the unions," the government officials said, "and soon all the poor in the country will be at our door. Western capitalists will grab the first plane to Tokyo, their suitcases stuffed with capital."

But very soon, a legitimate sense of pride prevailed. The government was happy to look so good to its electors. In 1969, Mr. Fukuda, the Minister of Finance, affirmed: "The Japanese will enjoy the highest per capita income in the world by 1990." Kahn had said: "by 2000 at the earliest; in 2010, at the latest." The devil take Kahn; from now on the Japanese would rely on their own statistics. The pessimists deserved to wear dunce caps.

Futurologists of every stripe—governmental, private, university—re-did Kahn's calculations. Anticipating the inevitable decline in expansion, and the effect of every conceivable unfavorable circumstance, they nevertheless confirmed Mr. Fukuda's prophecy. The figures—millions of tons, billions of dollars, trillions of yens—could send one spinning.

Here is how they arrived at their estimates: From 1970 to 1980, economic growth will average 11 percent per year. In the five-year period between 1968 and 1973, the gross national product will have doubled. According to the estimates of the Five Year Plan, in 1976 the national product would be 400 billion dollars, a revenue of $2,750 per person (allowing for an average rise of 4.4 percent in prices).

This would mean that in 1976 the Japanese economy would be as strong as that of France and West Germany put together; that Japan's per capita income would be superior to that of the major European countries; that the national product of 108 million Japanese inhabitants would be equivalent to that of all the countries of Asia together—including China—equal to the gross product of a billion and a half people. By 1980, Japan would pass the U.S.S.R. and become the second greatest economic power in the world. Then Japan would start her race with the United States, to arrive at Mr. Fukuda's rounded-out estimate of 1990.

"Watch out for the Nippons," the Europeans are beginning to say, even though up till recently they were spared the incursion of Japanese products into their markets. Europe, and especially France, have ignored this Asiatic giant in their commercial calculations. In 1969, the Common Market's trade with Japan represented only 1.9 percent of all trade outside the Community.

But soon there will be a veritable invasion of Japanese products into every crevice of Europe. Hundreds of thousands of Japanese representatives already circle the globe every year. The volume of Japanese foreign trade is going to quadruple by 1985. The projection for 1975 is 37 billion dollars. The Japanese merchant fleet is already the greatest; she should be able to reduce freight rates and enter every port in the world to unload products at unbeatable prices.

Japan has been asked to extend its foreign investments in developing and in rich countries. Subsidiaries or joint ventures will manufacture Japanese products on the spot. In Europe, the Japanese challenge could replace the American challenge.

Japan is already the principal supplier of the Far East. From Seoul to Djakarta, from Bangkok to Manila, bikes, motorcycles, trucks, cars, radios, and TV sets are all stamped *Made in Japan*. In the modern hotels in these capital cities, we amuse ourselves by discovering the origin of everything in the room: "Let's see if it's made in Japan." Almost everything—lamps, ventilators, air-conditioners, radios, drapes and spreads, china and ceramics, bathroom fittings—is.

The United States is the country most affected by this irresistible invasion. The U.S. absorbs one third of all of Japan's exports. American lobbies for steel, textiles, and electronics are all pacing the corridors of Washington trying to obtain some kind of protective duty. American textile factories are suffering. On the West Coast, the number of Japanese cars is impressive.

Europe is also affected; since Japanese products have captured the American market, European exports have suffered. American imports of German electronic products have fallen from 30 percent to 5 percent, to the great benefit of Japan, of course. Volkswagen loses its favorable position with Toyota and Nissan. Sales of Renaults and Simcas have also decreased.

As Japanese products improve in quality, they enter into formidable competition with European products. The Japanese have opened offices in the major cities of Europe—Paris, London, Brussels, Dusseldorf. From there, they make extensive surveys of the markets. Soon Japanese products will flood the European market, priced attractively in spite of customs duties.

The defeat suffered by Honda in 1968 due to poor service was nothing more than a pin prick. Nissan and Toyota, not easily discouraged, installed themselves in several European capitals to feel out the market with several thousands of vehicles. When the duty barriers are lowered, the dam will break.

Nissan has set up a huge assembly plant in Portugal. Honda won out over Fiat and Renault in Czechoslovakia to install a factory that produces 150,000 cars a year. No one is any longer surprised to see Japanese cars in the streets of Scandinavia, and in the streets of the Benelux countries.

You can even get scotch or spaghetti "made in Japan." A goodly part of the oysters that we eat come from Japanese beds. The Japanese control virtually all of the world's smoked salmon, sold under various brand names. They also dominate the European market for barbershop chairs through the intermediary of a firm with a Latin name. They sell watches to the Swiss, beer to the Germans, shoes to the Italians, tweeds to the English, boccie balls to the French, and even grass skirts to the Polynesians.

Electronicitis—The New Virus

To the Japanese, Europe appears old, tired, a civilization living off the glories of its past. No such nostalgia encumbers the Japanese. They live in the present, and refer always to the future. Being basically gregarious, practical, flexible, and highly mobile both geographically and socially, they do not fear the future.

The Osaka Exposition gave foreigners a stunning sample of some of the new inventions which the Japanese already take for granted—pocket telephone-television sets, a machine for men that washes, rinses, dries, and massages, employing ultrasonic waves.

There is talk of an electric newspaper where you choose the news area you are interested in by pushing a button, and then a receiver—no larger than a record player—types out the latest information on a kind of ticker tape. This gadget is already in the works.

In place of this mini-telex, Matsushita proposes a copying machine which plays through the ordinary TV set. A chemical firm is thinking of launching the plastic newspaper, which anyone can read at his leisure while taking his evening bath.

The present system of newspaper-making is already enough to stun the world. Completely automated rotary presses print 180,000 copies an hour. Pages composed in

Tokyo are transmitted to all the large cities, and printed almost instantly. National television programs are administered by computers: push a button and a card will give you your budget, the names of the producer and operator. The transmission of broadcasts by Radio Japan in some 15 foreign languages is entirely automated.

A revolution without precedent is planned in transportation. It grew out of the extraordinary concentration of population on the Pacific Coast. Toward 1985, 85 million people will live in a 1,250-mile-long ribbon of a city, stretching from Sapporo, the capital of the northern island of Hokkaido, to Fukuoka in the northern part of the southern island of Kyushu. This megalopolis is already a reality for more than half of its projected length, notably from Tokyo to Hiroshima. Along its way, there will be three enormous centers. Tokyo will have 33 million inhabitants; Osaka, 18 million; and Nagoya, 10 million. This urban band will be serviced by a spinal column of highways and railways, along which will be strung a pipeline of electric, telephonic, and computer cables. Total cost for the project: between 70 and 100 billion dollars.

The Tokaido line, presently being extended to Kobe and Yokohama, is but a fraction of what is envisioned for ultrarapid transit: computer driven trains going at 200 and 300 miles an hour. The linear train, with propulsion motors between the rails, is being tested. Rocket trains traveling on air cushions or on magnetic cushions are under study.

To connect Japan's islands, tunnels and suspended bridges will be built. A tunnel route and railway line two and a half miles long already exists between the isle of Kyushu and Honshu. A gigantic project, 22½ miles long, is in the process of penetrating between Honshu and Hokkaido under the strait of Tsugaru; it will be completed in a few years, maybe even before work on the tunnel under the English Channel is even begun. The interior sea between Honshu and Shikoku will be straddled by a colossal three-mile-long suspended bridge, the longest in the world. A dozen of these bridges will use up 2 million tons of steel, and will cost the fantastic sum of 4 billion dollars.

For the suburbs of Tokyo, which can extend up to 30 miles away from the work zone, Japanese planners foresee multiple networks of noiseless commuter trains which will travel at 100 miles an hour and cut present commuting time in half.

Since the Japanese are so short of living space, they plan more and more to use the ocean, not only to build island cities, but as a source of food. For centuries, the Japanese have used seaweed in their diet, and as a fertilizer. They are investigating new uses of the ocean's resources. Mitsubishi has already set up an underwater base for experimentation.

Islands, stolen from the sea, are being built more and more rapidly and cheaply, and industries are installed on these floating lands. They are reached by tankers of over 500,000 tons. Problems of health and safety of these coastal cities will have to be carefully regulated. Later, giant factories will desalinate the ocean water to provide the cities of the future with drinking water.

Floating neighborhoods will be built in shipyards and tugged out to sea to where they will be moored. The railways and highways reaching these islands will either float on the water, or be submerged in huge polyester tubes which will be laid under water, or dug out of the sea beds.

They adore new things. They have "electronicitis" in their bloodstream. The profusion of electric eyes, escalators, air-conditioners, closed-circuit televisions stupefies the visitor, but is considered quite banal by the Japanese. Everywhere elevators are automatic and kitchens are electrically

equipped. Guides couldn't function without megaphones
and walkie-talkies. Even lovemaking has its goodly share
of battery-operated gadgets.

It Is Already the Year 2000

For the time being, Tokyo is not beautiful; in fact, it is monstrous. But when the super-plan of airborne highways, skyscrapers, cross-ocean islands, and subterranean neighborhoods is realized, Tokyo might well be the futuristic dream city.

Up until very recently, the construction of skyscrapers was limited because of the danger of earthquakes. But thanks to modern techniques in engineering and technology, the Japanese are now able to plant lead pillars deep into the ground, and to build tall structures of extreme suppleness on these pillars—structures that will resist the most violent earth tremors. During the frequent quakes that disturb Tokyo, the upper stories of these buildings sway enough to give one vertigo. The newest of these structures will be a hotel of 1,100 rooms. It will stand 47 stories high.

A good portion of the capital already functions underground. Most modern buildings have two or three underground floors. In Tokyo, there are miles of subterranean stations, parking lots, galleries, banks, boutiques, and restaurants—some of them very luxurious—all copiously lit with neon. At midday, the whole city goes underground, strolling, eating, shopping, and banking. The Japanese counterpart to Maxim's of Paris is buried under the Sony Building. The underground Shinjuku station is as big as the Place de la Concorde; 2½ million passengers jam this station every day.

The most impressive underground complex is that of the Tokyo station, an edifice which spreads over 72,000 square yards and goes down four stories. At the bottom there is a subway. There is also an underground parking lot for 520 cars. On the first basement level, there are 350 stores, restaurants, and coffee shops, entwined in a labyrinth of avenues. Of course, all is air-conditioned and air-purified. The complex contains 6,000 fire extinguishers, its own fire department, and police force.

While Tokyo was digging these burrows, the overground city was not inconvenienced nor even aware of the project. The streets and sidewalks were replaced by portable steel plates which were removed at night when the derricks, cranes, and other equipment went to work.

The Osaka Expo also hinted at the kind of houses the Japanese will live in, in the year 2000. They will all be completely adaptable: They will be suitable for above ground, underwater, or underground living. They will be constructed of steel or plastic, or both; and they will be soundproof and odorproof. Some of these houses look like submarines with portholes; others look like soap bubbles. They will be mobile, so that they can be superimposed on each other like coral reefs, or lodged in steel cylinders, or suspended like giant mobiles. With these mobile, made-to-measure houses that can be easily taken from one city to another—from the bowels of the earth to the surface of the sea—the problem of housing will have been solved. Space in the air, underground, or undersea is practically infinite.

The architect Kurokawa, a close collaborator of Kenzo Tange, the mastermind of the Osaka Expo, explained his models to me. He said:

Tokyo will be a city of many levels superimposed on each other, with architecture and nature in complete harmony. The architecture must be dynamic. There will be method; but the composition will be free, as in music or mobile art. The houses will be mobile and interchangeable.

On land, houses must be imbedded in the earth. But on the water, it is easy to raise, dismount or move structures. This offers unlimited possibilities. All sorts of individual variations are possible.

The owners themselves will decide on the total configuration, and place their units wherever they wish. The units will be close to each other, but not contiguous.

Automobile traffic will not be prohibited. It will flow on circular highways girding the houses on the periphery; access from structure to structure is by automatic monorail suspended in air. Parks and green areas will exist on the water.

Here is one of my typical lodgings, exhibited at Osaka. This model includes a living area, a bedroom, a bathroom, and a kitchen. The unit is intended for one individual. For a couple, two units can be joined by a common bedroom. Once the honeymoon is over, it would be conceivable that the two units could be separated and could be available for new combinations. The units will be mass-

produced piece by piece. One will be able to purchase the type and number of pieces he chooses.

Rights of ownership and the right to make use of space must be clearly separated. Rights in space accrue to the State. This distinction, which I discussed at length with the government, will be formalized on a legal level in a few years. As for the ocean and the seas, the State is naturally the proprietor of these, and it alone will be empowered to dispense rights to utilization.

It will be big business that will blueprint the future, because their systems for decision-making are simple, and because their criteria are efficiency and profit-making. Big business will decide when to move from conception to experimentation, and from experimentation to production.

And they are already at the experimentation stage.

The Red Rays of the Rising Sun

*With the exception of the pygmies and
the Hottentots, the Japanese are, without
doubt, the least attractive race in the
world. The midgets of the East have
heads which are disproportionate to their
bodies, and faces which are expression-
less. . . .*

These remarks are taken from *Japan Unmasked*, a book
published in English by a Japanese, Ichiro Kawasaki, a
former Japanese ambassador to Argentina. Guilty of dero-
gating his countrymen before foreigners, he had to resign.

Still, some Japanese will openly admit that many of
their compatriots feel physically inferior to other races. However, since the war a more balanced diet has allowed the
Japanese to add an inch to their height, to put on a little
weight, and to improve their teeth. But when Japanese are
in the company of Caucasians, one gets the impression that
the Nippons are somewhat ill at ease. Before expansive
Westerners who are full of energy and freer in expressing
their emotions, the impersonal, timid, self-effacing Japanese
tend to be uncomfortable and mistrustful. Their history
attests to this; and in their daily life, a profusion of evidence
confirms the fact.

The White Complex

Ever since the Meiji regime, the Japanese national obsession has been to catch up with the Westerners. In 1905, the Japanese victory over Tsarist Russia was their first hour of glory. During Japan's conquering phase, her great wars could be interpreted as the revenge of a small, frustrated nation; the revenge of a country that felt insulted at world condemnation of her invasion of Manchuria, while at the same time, powerful European colonialists were flaunting their Asiatic conquests. Japan took revenge on whites living in Japan; they were arrested as spies and treated badly.

Japan's military particularly enjoyed taking revenge; their cynicism and brutality toward white prisoners betrayed a need to humiliate, which was only paralleled by German Nazis. Revenge was the one word found in all the newspapers of the period, the catch phrase of the "Chosen Race." The war in the Pacific was, without question, a racial war.

After Japan's defeat and her official *mea culpa*, the revenge became economic. At every step of the way, Japan has never ceased to systematically compare her economic achievements with those of the West. No other press in the world makes as much reference to foreigners. Should the statistics show the least gain in any sector, it will receive ample space; the least praise proffered to Japan is faithfully reported; if some dignitary arriving by plane at Haneda tells a journalist that Japan is a marvelous country, the entire press will proclaim his statement. Foreigners, and especially Americans, are quick to oblige with facile compliments in order to make their hosts swell with pride. The success of artistic, cultural, or fashion events seems to be judged by the number of Caucasians that were present.

The white foreigner is admired, imitated, flattered. He is always right. He is served before anyone else. One gives up one's seat on the train for him. One never dares tell him that the store is about to close. He is photographed, invited everywhere, permitted free entry to a movie or exhibition. I have witnessed a group of South Americans undress themselves down to the skin during a strip-poker game in a bar; the other customers pretended not to see, and the owner didn't dare ask them to put their clothes back on. During the Olympics in Tokyo, the French athletes complained about not having French programs and refused to use English programs; panic-stricken, the contrite Japanese begged a thousand pardons and scurried to print up new programs.

In business, one wouldn't dare overburden the honorable foreigner with work; one would never reproach him, even if that were justified; one pays through the nose to curry the favor of the foreigner. In the universities, even the most eminently qualified Japanese professor will be passed over in favor of a young foreigner without any particular competence. A foreigner may even demand a higher salary; and if he gives only half his lectures, no one would dare fire him.

Capitalizing on the Japanese admiration for Westerners, a foreigner who was no more than mediocre in his own country could, if he wished, easily become a personage of wealth and renown in Japan. As for the white woman, the Japanese tremble before her. They secretly observe her every move and gesture, while at the same time carefully avoiding her glance. They would not dare to offer her their gallant services, much less to court her.

But by and large, the Westerner is strictly to sell to.

The *gaijin* (Occidental) is the best publicity tool in Japan; on TV or in advertisements, a Caucasian guarantees the quality of the product. In store windows, mannequins always have European features. Brand names are written in Roman letters, and often are English sounding. Cigarettes are dubbed *Hi-Lite* or *Peace* or *Hope*. Cars are named *Bluebird, Crown, Cedric, Corona. Pioneer, Trio, Kenwood National* serve as monickers for hi-fi equipment. Beauty products bear French names. Manufacturers take full advantage of the fact that anything foreign, even if in name only, will attract buyers. The Japanese are virtually infatuated by European or American products, and regard them, on principle, as being of superior quality, which they often are. Domestic luxury items—beauty products, liquor, sports equipment—are the first to suffer.

Nostalgia for the Bowl of Rice

To travel abroad, to Europe or to North America, is the ambition of every Japanese. Travel allows him to satisfy his curiosity, and also bestows upon him considerable social prestige. For an artist, to exhibit or give a concert in Paris or New York is obvious proof of talent. For the architect, the doctor, or the hairdresser, a foreign degree is a symbol of competence.

Often, however, the Japanese is not enthralled by the trip of his dreams. The countries he visits are so different from his own, he feels completely lost. Timid, afraid of appearing ridiculous, deprived of any sense of initiative or humor, he doesn't know how to mix with others or how to make casual friends.

As a general rule, when he is outside of his environment, the Japanese does not assert himself; he transplants badly, and with a high degree of self-rejection. Abroad, he suffers from a too-rich diet, which in no time at all makes him yearn for his familiar bowl of rice. He spends lots of money and is often fooled (remember, he would not venture to protest). He tries to buy a little esteem by means of over-generous tips; he tries to make his hosts forget the drab country he comes from by showering them with gifts. Often the poor organization, filth, and negligent service of the hotels leave him with bad memories. Confronted by

English stuffiness, or French bad manners, or Italian excitability, or American familiarity, he feels his own differentness and he is delighted to return home, convinced that he is better off in Japan than anywhere else. The country the Japanese prefer above all others is Switzerland, undoubtedly because of its cleanliness and calm, and because it is so well organized for tourists. "Not a crevice," thought Tartarin, "that is not carefully swept."

The Japanese do not venture to travel outside their country except under the auspices of an organized tour. They are used to traveling in great numbers, visiting a dozen countries in 15 days, and seeing every one of the museums and historic monuments. Japanese who live abroad generally do not have much contact with the natives of that country. They move in their own circles, dining in Japanese restaurants where they meet their fellow countrymen. Students who study in foreign universities often return home without having made a single foreign friend. The one or two million emigrants, settled chiefly in Hawaii, Canada, California, and Brazil, live in their own villages or in their own quarters or communities. They are said to be calm, hard-working, and . . . different.

In international affairs, Japanese diplomats and representatives have the reputation of being taciturn, always smiling, dozing during sessions. They have very little impact; they do not even have their full share of members in the U.N. Secretariat, for example. They do not seek important offices, and are often outdistanced by their more aggressive colleagues. When participating in public functions, they prefer to serve in the research or statistical departments.

Buying International Prestige

"A merchant of transistors"—this was how de Gaulle described the former Prime Minister Ikeda after his visit to Paris. The Japanese were shocked, as revealed in their press. But their editorials acknowledged that the president of the French Republic was justified. The Japanese make excellent merchants, but poor diplomats. The Japanese are bitterly aware of this.

Shigeru Yoshida provided his country with brilliant leadership during the reconstruction that followed the war; and Mr. Sato commanded great respect in presiding over his country's growing prosperity after 1964. India had its Gandhi and Nehru, Indonesia had Sukarno, but Japan has not as yet produced a stellar political figure of international stature.

At international forums, Japanese representatives read stereotyped speeches, which for the most part, they themselves did not write. They hardly ever initiate a discussion. Japanese ambassadors serve primarily a commercial mission. Up to now, Tokyo has shown remarkable discretion on the international political scene. This political debility can be attributed to several causes—Japan's defeat, her construction which forbids her to play a strategic role, the distrust with which she is regarded by her former Asiatic victims, her alignment with the geopolitical policy of Washington, and above all, to her single-minded concentration on economics rather than politics. However, as she grows in stature industrially, political power will inevitably follow.

In any case, Japan seizes every opportunity to show off her economic strength and her restored pride. The poor countries of Asia admire her success, but it is praise from the rich countries that she seeks. No expense is spared in order to enhance national prestige.

The Japanese government is making great efforts to attract international conferences to its home grounds. It has even defrayed all the expenses for delegates and their secretaries, putting them up in the best hotels and showering them with gifts, just to be hospitable to "honorable foreigners" and to give them a chance to see Japan. Specialists of all kinds are invited to tour Japan at the expense of various government agencies or private firms. Many firms reserve large budgets for installing sumptuous offices in foreign capitals. The big newspapers maintain sizable staffs in these capitals.

In Japan the three major newspapers—*Mainichi, Yomiuri, Asahi*—print English editions even though they lose money on these editions. These editions are important because they are the primary source of information for foreign residents.

Japan's efforts to woo international acclaim started in 1964 with the Tokyo Olympics. For the first time, "the eyes of the world" were turned toward Japan, and everybody—architects, engineers, artists—exerted prodigious efforts to make the Olympics a smashing success. Tokyo was turned upside down. Broad avenues were constructed, and the transformation of the city was achieved. The Tokaido line was built in record time. "For the first time, some of our complexes vanished."

Some of the tourists who were interviewed said they

were more impressed by the customs of the country than by her technical feats. Because they had won the approval of the Caucasians, all of Japan suddenly determined to venerate its traditions, to mine its past. Young girls once more began to wear kimonos; old forgotten religious ceremonies were revived; artisans' crafts began to proliferate.

Hardly were the Olympics over, when Japan accepted the honor of hosting the international exposition of 1970. "Once again the entire world will focus on us," said Mr. Sato. "We must show them that we have become a modern, rich, and powerful nation." The government did not stint on expenses—it spent 2 billion dollars itself, out of the 2.8 billion dollar record cost of the Osaka Expo. More than 50 million people attended the exposition; but for Japan, the important visitors were the million foreigners.

In 1972, the winter Olympics took place at Sapporo. Mr. Sato's government pledged earlier that "Sapporo will surpass Grenoble from every point of view, including the culinary."

Japan has joined many international organizations, such as the Office of International Trade, the General Agreement on Tariffs and Trade, the Committee of European Economic Cooperation. She does not yet play an active role in these organizations, but the important thing is that she is present. She has asked for a seat on the Security Council of the U.N. This may be a premature wish, but Japan considers that her rank as third economic power in the world should earn her a place in the holy of holies.

Although Japan's political influence is not yet proportionate to her economic stature, she is beginning to come into her own. The U.S.S.R. would like to woo Japan away from the American orbit in order to have the Nippons as an ally against China. Russia may turn over to Japan the development of the immense area of Siberia. But Japan mistrusts Russia who, deep down, remains the traditional enemy.

The U.S. would like to share its responsibilities with Japan, and is waiting for Tokyo to relieve her of some of the burden of economic assistance to eastern Asia. The U.S. would like to have Japan as its partner in its grand strategy in the Pacific. In 1969, Mr. Sato agreed to consider Japan co-responsible for the security of South Korea and Formosa.

But it is among her immediate neighbors in Asia that Japan really cuts a grand figure. Her economic power has made her the lordly master of the entire region.

The Yellow Yankees

If the Japanese feel a sense of inferiority toward the white race and constantly compensate for it, they feel a distinct sense of superiority toward all other people of the yellow race. Although this superiority would seem to be well justified by the enormous wealth of the Japanese, one nevertheless wonders if it does not in fact cover up an inferiority complex. The Japanese are no more comfortable with other Asiatics than they are with whites.

Except from the viewpoint of potential business, the Japanese are not at all curious about other Asian countries. If a Nippon is able to travel, he will choose a Western country. At the very most, he will spend a day or two in Hong Kong or in Bangkok. But he would never think of spending all of his vacation time to become better acquainted with one of his neighbors, even though the temples of Angkor or the enchanting island of Bali are closer and cheaper to get to.

Japanese businessmen or technicians who travel or live in other countries of the Orient often betray their basic attitude of disdain and arrogance in their manner toward the people of their host country. The Japanese seem to despise their Asian brothers because of their poverty, and they are absolutely horrified by the filth other Eastern countries easily tolerate. They abhor the casual dishonesty with which crafty Chinese or Indian merchants try to extract from them twice as much as they should. They seem to be disconcerted by the quick minds of the Chinese; they are irritated by the self-assurance of the Thais; jealous of the Latin exuberance of the Filipinos; and envious of the serene indolence of the Malaysians.

The Japanese seldom bother to learn the language of the country they live in; business transactions have to be carried on in English or, better yet, in Japanese. "After all," they say, "it is up to the weaker to learn the language of the stronger."

In the capital cities of Asia, the Japanese monopolize the golf clubs and the most luxurious restaurants. Even when they want to establish human contact with the local people they are awkward at it; they simply do not know how to make themselves popular. Apart from the merchants, who thrive on the Japanese mania for collecting souvenirs, and the waiters who enjoy their lavish tips, all over, in Jakarta and Singapore, in Saigon and Manila, everyone agrees: The Japanese have not made themselves particularly well liked. They are still heartily detested in Korea where they had made fierce attempts at colonization.

In Korea, as well as in Formosa, the Japanese—who do not appreciate being reminded of the debt they owe the Chinese and Korean civilizations—did everything they could to destroy the very souls of the people they enslaved. The Koreans and the Formosans were not allowed to observe their traditions, nor to use their own language. It was obligatory to learn Japanese. Disobedience of the slightest nature was punishable by death. The Koreans were treated as slaves. Forty or fifty thousand of them were imported to Japan and used as forced labor in the mines. Today, these displaced persons and their descendants constitute a colony of six hundred thousand. They are still despised as inferiors.

In his film *The Hanging,* the director Oshima magnificently depicted the racism of the Japanese in relation to the people of Chosen.

The armed Japanese who invaded Southeastern Asia on the pretext of liberating that area from the oppression of the whites conducted themselves with incredible brutality. The memory of their arrogance and of their merciless domination remain vivid down to this very day.

In consequence, the peoples of East Asia do not feel much affection for their rich neighbor in the north. They regard with distrust her newly found power and her ever-growing ambitions. They know the dangers of becoming involved in business connections with Japan, since they are aware of the fact that the Japanese are not in the habit of being altruistic. Her very presence provokes a nagging fear of military intervention. They bitterly affirm that Japanese businessmen who work in their countries never hire indigenous workers for any important position, however qualified a native might be. These attitudes and tactics have earned the Japanese the nickname of "Yellow Yankees." Their fellow Asians say the Nippons intend to obtain with dollars what they were unable to obtain with arms.

But whether they like it or not, these countries must relate to their detested enemy of yesterday. Their development depends on Japan's prosperity. As for Japan, she needs her neighbors in order to guarantee her own continuous expansion. For the time being, common interests irrevocably draw Japan and her Asian neighbors together.

Japan has attempted to reconcile her ex-victims by continuing to pay enormous war reparations. In Tokyo, where they do not like the expression one bit, these reparations pass under the euphemism of "economic assistance." Since the beginning of the 60's, Japanese diplomats in Asia have deployed an intensive offensive of smiles and generosity.

Eastern ministers and heads of state invited to Tokyo rarely leave without carrying away as gifts proposals for projects or other assistance.

In 1967, Mr. Sato made an unprecedented tour of the Eastern Asiatic countries, including Burma. He pledged Japan to substantial economic aid, and he was well received everywhere.

Tutor to Asia

In all the capitals of the Far East, enormous neon signs decorate the tallest buildings; these are almost always Japanese ads. It is very disturbing to see these monstrosities desecrating the most peaceful horizons, defiling the most charming quarters. These luminous masses of capitalistic advertising destroy the harmonious arrangement of tall white buildings rising like graceful organ pipes on Victoria Isle in Hong Kong; they aggressively insinuate themselves between the minarets and palm trees in Kuala Lumpur, and loom hideously in the sky at Taipei. Large Japanese stores in Bangkok, Hong Kong, and Manila acquaint the Thais, the Chinese, and the Filipinos with the riches of the Japanese consumer society. Japanese businessmen ply the Far Eastern capitals—their objective: the Japanization of the Orient.

Japan has become the major business partner of the countries of East Asia, absorbing a third of the exports from these countries. In the Philippines, Japan has displaced the United States; in Australia or Malaysia, Japan has superseded England. Japan acquires a good part of its raw materials from these Asiatic countries. And the money she spends for these raw materials ends up right back in her own pocket as Asians buy the Japanese-made finished products.

Large Japanese companies have subsidiaries in South Korea, in Formosa and in Hong Kong, and profit immensely from the cheap labor there. But the countries benefit too: now Indonesia has an oil refinery in Sumatra; there are steel mills in Malaysia and Formosa; Singapore has a large shipyard for naval repairs. Korea, Thailand, Formosa, as well as Australia, New Zealand, and Canada assemble Japanese cars. Japanese business joins with local capital and spreads the Japanese know-how.

Japanese aid to underdeveloped countries grows larger every year. In 1968, such aid totaled a billion dollars. It is true, of course, that the credit for importation of Japanese products accounts for more than half that figure, and direct investment accounts for hardly more than a tenth (of which the government's share is only a third). Outright gifts are relatively parsimonious, and credit terms are stricter than those of other purveyors of aid. Nevertheless, Japan is now in fourth place among the countries extending aid, behind the United States, France, and Western Germany. In 1968, .74 percent of Japan's gross national product was devoted to such aid, which is less than the one percent recommended by the O.C.D.E. for third-world contributions; but the amount is rising steadily. Japan has promised at least 2 billion dollars for aid in 1975. Loans from Japan contributed not inconsiderably to the economic growth of such countries as South Korea and Formosa; loans from the Japanese government to these two countries exceeded a billion dollars. Japanese loans also helped President Suharto rescue Indonesia from the complete shambles into which Sukarno had delivered it.

During the last years, something has become clear to Japanese business and government leaders: the close geographic and economic solidarity that unites the dwellers in the Pacific—Australia, New Zealand, South Eastern Asia, Burma, Formosa, South Korea; and, on the other side of the Pacific—Canada and the United States. These absorb close to 80 percent of Japan's exports. They also furnish two thirds of her imports. Alaska, with her forests, fisheries, and especially her petroleum, looks increasingly to Japan to export to. Japan now gives considerable thought to the Asian-Pacific zone, assuming Tokyo to be its center. It is in this zone that Japan's ambition for the future lies.

Japan shares political interests, as well as economic, with the developed countries of this Asian-Pacific region. She forms a *de facto* "rich man's club" with Australia, New Zealand, Canada, and the U.S. Japan is interested in co-ordinating the cooperation of all the members of this elite group with respect to the disinherited countries of the Western Pacific. She would, of course, be the first to profit from such cooperation.

Establishing a firmer community is even more important since two new political factors have entered the scene and created a void in Southeast Asia. First, excluding Hong Kong, there is the imminent removal of all British forces from East of Suez, which means from Singapore and Malaysia. Secondly, there is the progressive withdrawal of American forces from Guam as announced by President Nixon in 1969. Japan holds an important card which it can play here—not necessarily a political card, but an economic ace. Tokyo believes that there is no better rampart against communism than wealth.

International organizations have been established throughout the countries of Southeast Asia. Japanese businessmen were the first apostles of these organizations, and formed, together with Australia, New Zealand, and Canada, a Committee for Cooperation in the Pacific basin. A development bank was initiated (Japan's contribution of 200 million dollars equaled that of the United States) with its center in Manila. Its projects for developing the poor countries of Asia will be accelerated by the formation of an association of private bankers to seek out profitable investment ventures.

The Asian Pacific Council is one of the major political organs, and Japan is its prime mover. This organization is not running smoothly as yet, since some of the members—notably South Korea and Formosa—want to use the organization as an anti-communist vehicle. Japan refuses to get involved in these games. She does not approve of Washington's policy of the containment of China. To Tokyo, Peking is not an enemy; on the contrary, they will someday become close partners.

700 Million Chinese

Japan does not recognize Communist China. Officially, she ignores the 700 million Chinese who live opposite her. This would appear to be an aberration, and no one would agree more than the Japanese government. But there are two obstacles to recognition: First, there is Japan's diplomatic alignment with United States diplomacy; and there is Japan's participation in the American security system in the Far East, through her allowing American bases on her territory.

But the second obstacle is the more important one: Recognition of Chaing Kai-shek's tiny Nationalist China (15 million inhabitants) precludes serious reconciliation with Peking. Japan's trade with Nationalist China (800 million dollars in 1969) is more important than her trade with Communist China (625 million dollars in 1969).

Another important reason for the loyalty of the Japanese toward the Chinese of Taipei is that Chiang Kai-shek renounced war reparations. Peking did not do so. Obviously, the reparations that could be claimed would be enormous: Massacres committed by Japanese troops caused at least 12 million deaths, and the bomb damage was devastating.

The military strength of China does not disturb Japan. The West tends to exaggerate the panic which is supposed to prevail at each new exploit on the part of Chinese scientists experimenting with atoms and rockets. In fact, Chinese explosions, and their recent launching of a satellite which showed that they will soon be able to command long range rockets, did not cause the Japanese to turn a hair. The Japanese know that China has nuclear arms, which they regard as defensive only. They judge that, unless provoked, China is not an aggressive nation; at least, she has never been throughout her history. On the contrary, it was China that submitted to invasions by Mongols, Manchurians, and Japanese. China's intervention in Korea in 1950 was caused by the extreme pressure of having American troops at her Yalu border.

China has never attacked Japan. Since the war, it was the Japanese official observers and newspaper correspondents who were the least alarmist and who gave China the most objective and sympathetic coverage. Actually, the Japanese harbor a secret admiration for China, the mother of their own civilization.

And, of course, Japan is best situated to conquer the fabulous market that 700 million Chinese project. Many businessmen, supported by liberal factions within the Conservative party and by parties of the opposition, are more insistently demanding the recognition of Peking. For the government, this is impossible at the present time; but even Mr. Sato, who heads the most conservative elements in his party, hopes for a "a normalization of relations between the two countries," based on the sacrosanct principles of the separation of economic and political interests.

Peking regularly heaps insults upon Japan, accusing her of being the imperialistic lackey of America, of collusion with Russia, of pillaging the resources of Southeast Asia, and of promoting her own dormant militarism. But these are mere verbal barrages. The situation was more realistically summarized by Premier Chou En-Lai who declared to a Japanese economic mission in April, 1970, that "the big obstacle to the re-establishment of normal relations between China and Japan is Formosa." The Chinese showed in many subtle and some less subtle ways that they do not want to burn the bridges between themselves and the Japanese. They are far from bearing toward their ex-enemy the kind of distrust that Poland bears for Germany, for example. Neither Peking nor Tokyo wants to sacrifice trade to politics, especially since the amount of trade is substantial.

China is Japan's fourth largest supplier, and Japan is China's best customer. Semi-official exchanges are still quite feeble. The important trade is carried on by "friendly" firms, whose representatives go through a customary charade: They carry in their pockets a copy of the little red book of the thoughts of Mao, and begin every business discussion with the toast, "Long live President Mao," and end the discussion with, "Down with Japanese imperialism." Japanese businessmen circulate in fairly large numbers in Peking, Shanghai, and Canton, and also attend all the trade fairs.

Tokyo is waiting for the day when the conflict in Vietnam finally draws to an end, and for the day when China resolves its enormous internal problems. Japan secretly hopes for the end of both the regime of Mao and that of Chiang Kai-shek, after which anything will be possible.

"The Chosen Race"

Since 1969-1970, the roofs of Tokyo have been bedecked with flags. This is a relatively new phenomenon. Previously, these banners made their discreet appearances on the occasion of a national holiday. Now the red emblem of the Eastern sun floats permanently on high atop stores, hotels, and other buildings, symbolizing the resurgence of a nationalism that was never really extinguished.

Japan is fully aware of its role in the murderous World War II, but the patriotism manifesting itself today has taken on a new hue: Economists have replaced the generals. Japan keeps reminding itself that today it is no longer a military power, but has become an outstanding economic power. A great deal of energy is expended to persuade the entire country that they are a nation of élite. This campaign seems to be succeeding in relieving the inferiority complex from which the Japanese have suffered.

In 1953, a national poll posed the question: "Do you consider yourself superior or inferior to the Westerners?" Twenty percent responded *Superior;* and 28 percent responded *Inferior.* To the same question posed in 1968, 47 percent responded *Superior,* and 12 percent responded *Inferior.*

The newly found pride of the Japanese was so ubiquitously displayed at the Osaka exposition that it seemed to be more of a Japanese exposition than an international one. It was, indeed, a Japanese industrial fair, if one were to judge by the numerous pavilions displaying the strength of the industrial empire.

With very rare exceptions, the Japanese more than love their country—they adore and worship it. They extol its uniqueness, its landscapes, its people and products. Their patriotism reaches cult proportions.

The Japanese love and admire each other. If they have been through the "terrible foreign experience," they console each other with: "Nothing-is-as-good-as-the-company-of-another-Japanese." They are convinced that their way of life is the most agreeable. But to a Westerner, the ugliness and the filthy atmosphere of big Japanese cities (where most Japanese live), make even cities like Los Angeles, New York, Paris, and Liverpool seem, in contrast, like peaceful havens.

The average Japanese is sincerely convinced he belongs to the most interesting nation in the world, the one with the richest traditions. But when one realizes how thoroughly they have denigrated their past, and sees to what extent they have embalmed their traditions under plastic and neon, one is dismayed by the spiritual poverty of the country.

Betimes, Japanese nationalism takes on a racist slant. Gone are the days when the Japanese expressed sincere guilt and manifested a sincere desire to make moral and financial restitution to the Asiatics they had invaded and oppressed. It is becoming more and more evident that the purveyors of Japanese aid have only contempt for the "incompetent races" they are so "generously helping."

This contempt extends to the half-Japanese half-Caucasian Nisei. When the Japanese speak of Nisei it sounds as if the word is synonymous with "bastard." After the war, a number of Nisei left California to live in Japan. Under the

American Occupation, they found no difficulty in getting work. But after the Occupation, especially in executive jobs in industry and government, they realized that there was a level beyond which they would not be allowed to go. Nisei I have known have confided to me that they feel ostracized. Nisei, born after the war to Japanese mothers and American GI's, have had great difficulty being accepted in Japanese society; while those unfortunate enough to have had a black father don't stand a chance of being integrated. A Japanese who lives with a white is considered a renegade.

Mishima and his Private Army

Japanese nationalism sometimes displays a petty meanness. In June, 1968, after exercising protectorship for 23 years, the United States returned to Japan the Bonin archipelago, on which is situated the island of Iwo Jima, the site of one of the most bloody battles of the Pacific—6,000 American soldiers were slain, and 22,000 Japanese defenders chose to fight to the death or to commit suicide rather than surrender. The American government was asked to remove the Stars and Stripes that floated above the monument honoring the brave American marines and was authorized to replace it with a metal flag. But the size of this copper copy of the American flag caused bitter controversy in Tokyo. After much discussion, the Japanese government asked the United States to reduce the size of its emblem. To subdue outraged public opinion, Japan decided to erect opposite the American monument, a majestic memorial honoring the Japanese heroes.

This action did not seem to me to be an attempt to get back at their former conqueror, but was rather a skin-deep manifestation of nationalism. To the extent that such demonstrations increase, they risk reawakening ancient xenophobic feelings.

A special government mission was created to call to the attention of foreign publishers the errors that appeared in

their works about Japan, and the ministry of education rewrote certain pages of Japanese history. Mythology was
restored to its honorable position; the Manchurian incident
that precipitated the invasion of China, and the initiation
of the war in the Pacific were reviewed. A Professor Ienaga
attacked the Ministry of Education for wanting to impose on
him some 200 revisions before he would be allowed to publish his history manual. Justifying his action, the minister
averred, "One must not destroy the national sense of identity." Greatly encouraged, pressure groups of rightist per-
suasion waged a campaign to restore in the schools lessons
in *shushin,* the traditional pre-war code of ethics.

Traditional morality has become the subject of much
discussion among people and in the newspapers. Premier
Sato made a pronouncement in 1968 which he has repeated
on many other occasions, and which has had profound re-
percussions: "The development of national (or nationalistic)
sentiment emerges as the most pressing task."

Nationalistic right wing organizations are growing in
number and power every day. They demand priority for rearmament. Highly placed members of business and government, such as former Prime Minister Kishi and Mr.
Kaya, finance minister at the time of Pearl Harbor, support
these organizations covertly and sometimes overtly.

While it is true that extreme right wing adherents represent but a small minority of the population, they are a
noisy minority and not at all timid about when and where
to spread their propaganda. The police do not interfere with
them. The membership remains secret; but it is suspected
that some of their members were former high-ranking officers and officials during Japan's colonizing days. Let me add,
without drawing too hasty conclusions, that some of those,
who were purged by the Americans after the war for having
been party to Japan's militarism, have been reinstated in

important administrative, political, and economic posts. The most outstanding example of this is the case of Mr. Kishi, minister of armaments in the war cabinet of General Tojo. He was imprisoned from 1945 to 1948 as a war criminal, but this didn't stop him from serving as prime minister from 1957 to 1960. He still wields enormous political power behind the scenes; his brother, Mr. Sato, is the current prime minister. In the October, 1952 elections, held six months after the San Francisco peace treaty went into effect, 130 people purged by the occupation authorities were elected to the Diet; they constituted a third of the new Assembly.

Before his suicide in 1971, the writer Yukio Mishima, who was runner-up for the Nobel Prize for Literature in 1968, was considered to hold opinions somewhere between the conservative right and the extreme right. Mishima maintained that only through a return to the great traditions of the past could Japan be saved from decadence. He extolled the cult of the emperor, and wanted to restore both the code of honor of the samurai and the purifying value of hara-kiri. With his troupe of a dozen or so samurai-militants, Mishima held regular training sessions, and organized mini-parades to which the press was invited. His flag featured the pre-war imperialistic symbol of the red rays around the rising sun. His enemies, and others jealous of his popularity, made fun of him, and called him the "commander of an army of pederasts."

But many Japanese applauded the "symbolic value" of his crusade. Mishima attempted a minor—almost symbolic —coup d'état, and then atoned for his failure and brought world attention to his movement by committing public hara-kiri.

Today, about 20 million Japanese adhere to diverse religious doctrines, all fairly recent in origin and very nationalistic in orientation. The Kurozumikyo has a million followers and preaches the return to mythological sources, notably the cult of the sun goddess Amaterasu. The Tenrikyo, "the religion of divine wisdom," ordains as one of its principal commandments the veneration of the emperor and the exaltation of the fatherland.

But by far the most important and the most alarming of the modern mystical sects is that of the Soka Gakkai.

An Electronic Beadle

Founded in 1930, the Soka Gakkai has met with fantastic success during the last ten years. The Soka Gakkai maintains it has converted 7 million families (they recruit by families). Observers of the movement would place their number today somewhere between 10 and 15 million people.

The Soka Gakkai doctrine of a society that is a creator of values was based on the teachings of Nichiren, a 13th-century monk. Nichiren was a strange sort of Buddhist and the most fanatic patriot Japan has ever known. He claimed to be the sole possessor of Buddhist truth and preached that Japan would spread this true Buddhism throughout the world. Today, the Soka Gakkai harbor the same sentiments, more subtly and discreetly perhaps, but no less moderately.

Unlike the other Japanese religions, the Soka Gakkai feels the call to proselytize all over the world. It has a network of recruiting missions spread over all five continents. The sect is particularly active in Korea and in the U.S. A large number of their American followers were converted in Japan, where as lonely souls in American bases, they sought an exotic mystique or a way of penetrating the sealed Japanese society and were seduced by these persuasive, dedicated people who talked about the world being "one large family."

Their methods for conversion are aggressive. Small groups of "commando" missionaries politely edge their way into homes and proceed to actively "soul wash." If they arouse interest, they will return again and again, until their task is accomplished. When they are successful, they provide the family with an altar complete with directions for use. The converted learn that one of their main religious duties is to constantly preach the new gospel to their family, friends, and neighbors.

The method of recruitment is well organized. Every year, a goal for new converts is fixed by the general staff, territories are laid out, and techniques are discussed. Then the crusade beings. The goals were set with an eye toward success, and they generally are achieved.

Converts are mainly recruited from the lower classes and the disinherited: the retired, the widowed, the peasants, the poor artisans, the employees in small factories, the dayworkers—all are choice prey. To all these little people, the sect offers a "family," financial assistance, and moral comfort—these are the magnets. This social base of the Soka Gakkai strikingly calls to mind the people that made Hitler and Mussolini so successful; no small wonder that the Soka Gakkai is often labeled fascist.

The method is very simple. Sacred texts and litanies are invoked as often as possible. Daily prayers in the home are obligatory, as well as regular attendance at the temple. Mass pilgrimages to places holy to the sect are highly recommended. Some of these pagodas are ultramodern structures. On a television screen, a beadle watches to see that the ceremony is proceeding properly. He regulates the liturgy by pushing buttons on a dashboard; he achieves lighting effects by regulating lanterns and floodlights; he controls the automatic opening and closing of doors and curtains; he bangs the gong and sounds the bells, all without ever leaving his post; such are the miracles of electronically aided prayer.

After the service, the congregation, worn out by the interminable murmuring of incantations, retires to the cafeteria in the temple for refreshments. Over a cup of coffee, they discuss the latest pronouncements of President Ikeda with their pastors who are still bedecked in their ceremonial dress. Endowed with a halo of quasi-divine prestige, President Ikeda is the patron saint of the Soka Gakkai.

Members of the sect are encouraged to meet regularly in their neighborhoods. The atmosphere at these meetings is a mixture of kindergarten, communist cell, parish council. The moral climate is frankly puritan; young parishioners are not the least bit frivolous or flirtatious; mini-skirts for girls and long hair for boys are forbidden.

Governing about 12 million people, the sect has become a powerful secular as well as spiritual force. The Soka Gakkai forms a kind of state within a state. They have their own schools, and they will soon have their own university. They render many social services to their members. They have begun to organize a union of small workers, called Minro, which employers will soon have to start taking seriously. Their women's groups include millions of members. The vitality of their newspapers and magazines is impressive. They have several dailies—the most important one prints 1,100,000 copies; weeklies; and monthlies—the largest of these circulates 2 million copies. They also print millions of books in their own publishing houses. Their press proclaims the glories of the historic mission of the Soka Gakkai, as well as its present accomplishments. It extols President Ikeda exactly as the Chinese press does with respect to President Mao; the name of the well-loved leader and his thoughts are endlessly repeated, his activities diligently made known.

The Soka Gakkai sect also has an extensive cultural program; their popular Concert Association has almost 2 million subscribers; their theatrical group encompasses 100,000 regular participants. From time to time they will present giant shows in huge stadiums to impress infidels with their power and talent. There are choirs and ballet dances with thousands of participants. Their panoramic stagecraft cannot help remind one of the parades of Mussolini and Hitler.

What they aspire to, of course, is political power. Their members, often key figures in local assemblies, sometimes monopolize these local governing agencies. On the national scale, they have forged a political arm, the Komeito, the party of "the golden mean." Its opening gun was to propose ten candidates for the upper House—they were all elected. In January, 1967, they had their first slate of candidates in the general election—out of 32 candidates, 25 were elected. In the December, 1969 elections, they doubled the number of seats they held (from 25 to 47) and they are now the second party of the opposition after the Socialist party. The Komeito is moving slowly but surely.

The Soka Gakkai are convinced that in the next 10 years they will become the most important opposition party, and that they will take over the government one day, sharing it if necessary with the conservatives. Will this come to pass? Most Japanese do not think so, and in fact prefer not to think about it at all.

Domestically, the program of the Komeito caters to the needs of housewives and poor people. It strongly censures corruption. In foreign politics, it strongly supports a policy of neutralism. But recently the Komeito committed a serious error which marred its reputation for honesty and showed that it had a rather strange idea about democratic freedom. A professor of political science, Hirotatsu Fujiwara, wrote a book, *The Real Face of the Soka Gakkai,* revealing the fascist coloration of the sect. The author committed the "unpardonable sacrilege of daring to criticize President Ikeda." Everything imaginable was done to keep the book from being published. Bribes and threats of blackmail were sent to the editors who backed down, one after the other. Offers of fabulous sums were made to the author to pressure him into renouncing the book or to at least revise it. Pressure of all kind was put on top politicians, and this might have worked if Premier Sato, himself, had not refused to go along. Finally, despite all, the book was published, and the Komeito was dealt a severe blow. Its opponents did not fail to exploit the scandal for all it was worth.

You either like the Soka Gakkai and join the sect, or you hate and fear it. Their enemies denounce their fascist character, insidious propaganda, excessive puritanism, arrogance, and fanatical patriotism. When one understands the methods of this politico-religious sect and the composition of its social base, one cannot help but think that under its sweet, obsequious exterior, it is a potentially dangerous force. What would happen if, one day, Japan ran into an economic crisis serious enough to shake up the essentially passive population, whose nationalism is fanatical, and whose respect for force is absolute? One remembers how fascism took over in Italy and Germany.

Okinawa

The Japanese are becoming more and more sensitive about their national image. They no longer tolerate having some of their territory occupied by former conquerors, American or Russian. In 1966, the Japanese government raised the problem of taking back the Bonin Islands and Okinawa. These had been under U.S. control since the war. The government began an important press campaign to excite public opinion on the subject. Not one day passed without the press bringing up the lost and longed for islands. "The restitution of Okinawa to the mother country" became the battle cry from all directions; and over a period of three years that slogan brought millions of people into the streets in demonstrations.

In November of 1967, as a gesture of appeasement, the U.S. agreed to turn over Iwo Jima and the Bonins to Japan. The U.S. hoped that this good-will gesture—cheap enough, since the places are of no strategic value whatsoever—would quiet things down. But it only whet the Japanese appetite. Okinawa, the scene of the most vicious battle in the Pacific war, was the real issue. Thirteen thousand Americans fell to conquer that island, as did innumerable kamikaze pilots. It was on Okinawa that the Americans realized the extent of Japan's commitment to victory. It was clear that the Japanese soldiers would fight to the last, that civilians would do battle with bamboo sticks if they had to, that the women and children who were taken prisoner would carry grenades in their hands. It was here, no doubt, that America realized that nothing short of an atomic blood bath would fell Japan.

Ever since 1945, Okinawa, with its one million inhabitants, its 117 bases and military installations, its arsenal of atomic warheads, and its 50,000 soldiers, has been the key area in the American defense system in East Asia. In the Vietnam war, Okinawa became the prime relay point, the principal logistic center, a chief training area, and a B-52 airbase.

Encouraged rather than appeased by the return of Iwo Jima, the campaign for the restitution of Okinawa intensified. Mr. Sato had no choice but to support it. He declared that he would "gamble his career on the disappearance of these last vestiges of defeat."

Washington realized that Okinawa had become a very serious issue and could compromise its relations with its most faithful ally. In November, 1969, President Nixon gave his promise to Mr. Sato to return Okinawa to Japan in 1972.

Tokyo then shifted its campaign for recouping territories to the north, to the Kurile Islands. Here the diplomatic enemy is Russia. The Japanese demand the restitution of two tiny islands, Habomai and Shikotan, and of two of the bigger Kurile Islands, Kunashiri and Etorofu. The Soviets have occupied these islands since 1945, and Etorofu has become one of their important military bases.

From the Russian point of view there is no issue: Those islands now belong to them. Japan implicitly renounced them when she signed her own separate peace treaty with the United States in San Francisco in 1951. The most the Russians would agree to would be to return the two small fishing islands, Habomai and Shikotan, when the Japanese sign a peace treaty with Russia.

But the Japanese are very obstinate. All the Russian refusals would not succeed in diminishing their campaign. On official Japanese maps, the southern Kuriles are shown as part of the mother country. The press conscientiously publishes every detail of the Japanese-Russian negotiations. Japanese businessmen precede every contract negotiation with the Russians with a little prologue concerning the islands. For the Japanese government, the campaign "to return to the mother countries the northern territories" has a great advantage: It is a great boost to national pride. Even the Japanese Communist party, the Socialist party, and the Komeito approve the government's position and support a return to the 1875 borders.

There are few Pacific coastlines in the world who are untroubled by Japanese fishing boats intruding into their territorial waters. Russia has boarded over a thousand such craft. Indonesia, and Malaysia, and countries on the American continent that border on the Pacific, continually protest to the Japanese government on the subject. But the Japanese press treats the news of the boarding of trawlers and the arrest of their seamen as another national insult and an outrage.

When the Russians imprisoned some Japanese fishermen in 1968, the Japanese Minister of Agriculture, Kuraishi, announced that, in order to protect its nationals, Japan should develop its navy and equip itself with nuclear armaments. It is true that an outcry of opposition forced Mr. Kuraishi to resign, but it has been said that he only voiced out loud what many really think in secret.

Anything that affects her nationals outside her frontiers is of tremendous importance for Japan. Their feelings are easily hurt. The least affront by a foreigner to the most minor Japanese official if reported by the Japanese press could incite a national furor. During the 1968 Tet offensive in South

Vietnam, the Japanese press told the story of a heroic Japanese business agent in Saigon: The poor man couldn't buy cabbages because they had become too expensive and had "to survive for several days on only two meals a day." The government considered recalling all its nationals living in Saigon.

This unimportant anecdote allows me the opportunity to propose a hypothesis that is food for thought. Supposing that in one of the Asiatic countries where the Japanese are not very well liked, such as the Philippines, an incident were to erupt between a Japanese and a native; supposing that it culminated in the murder of a technician or of a businessman, and the safety of other Japanese were seriously endangered; and the local powers did nothing to intervene—what would Tokyo's reaction be? Would she send over one of her naval units to take back her nationals? Not necessarily; but once the humiliation-hatred network is sparked off, very serious consequences could follow.

The Switzerland of the East

The Japanese constantly take pleasure in saying that their country is the most peaceful in the world. They swear that the war and their defeat have given them a profound and permanent distaste for arms and violence. They point out that their country spends proportionally less on defense than any other polity in the world.

MacArthur wanted to make Japan the Switzerland of the East. He gave her a pacifist constitution which in Article Nine had her renounce war forever and prohibited her from having armed forces.

In June, 1950, the Korean War breaks out. From one day to the next, the U.S. changes policy. John Foster Dulles goes to Tokyo and blithely asks Yoshida to rearm. The Prime Minister grins under his lorgnette. He slides under the eyes of the American Secretary of State the Japanese constitution, and points to Article Nine. Dulles becomes furious. He slams his fist down on the table and bellows: "You MUST rearm." Finally, Yoshida consents to creating a small "security force" of 75,000 guardsmen.

Today, Article Nine of the Japanese constitution is a quaint anachronism. The security force Dulles was so anxious to create was the embryo of the present Japanese Army.

The beautiful pacifist ideal allowed Japan to devote all its money to the reconstruction of the country. It is easy to renounce arms when there is no menace.

The Japanese American Defense Treaty of September 8, 1951, signed at the same time as the peace treaty at San Francisco, turned the occupiers of Japan into her allies. The U.S. covered Japan with her nuclear umbrella, and guarded her bases. In 1970, there were still close to 150 U.S. bases in Japan manned by 45,000 American soldiers.

In 1960, the revision of the defense treaty was accompanied by a series of blunders on the part of Prime Minister Kishi. Popular protest caused his downfall. But ten years later, in 1970, the treaty was tacitly approved. Aside from a few students and left wingers, nobody protested. Polls indicated that the majority of the Japanese people approve the alliance with the U.S., which does not stop them from illogically but patriotically complaining, at one and the same time, about the presence of American bases on their territory. The Japanese were very happy to have American protection because it permitted them to serenely concentrate on their economic development, despite the war in Korea, despite the cold war, despite the proximity of the two great nuclear powers, Russia and China.

But this situation could not go on forever. For the last few years, Washington has been pressing Tokyo to become wholly responsible for her own defense, and to share responsibility for the defense of the rest of the Far East. Okinawa furnished Nixon with another lever to force Tokyo to start acting like a major political ally. Nixon promised to return Okinawa to Japan; but in exchange, insisted that Japan accelerate its own rearmament and participate in the U.S. strategy in Asia. This implies that Japan will let the U.S. use her military bases should offensive action in the Far East be necessary. This further implies that Japan will consider her own security closely tied to the security of South Korea and Formosa.

Japan bought the deal. Peking, Pyongyang, and Moscow fumed. But Sato felt he had no choice. For him, this agreement offered the long-awaited opportunity to destroy the legend that Japan is nothing more than an economic being. To make the country a political and strategic power, it would be necessary to provide an army.

In 1968, General de Gaulle told the national Institute of Higher Studies of Defense that Japan was not a political power because it was not a military force. This remark made a forcible impression on the Japanese. Today they have resigned themselves to the inevitable: They have decided to become a great power.

Hiroshima Is Forgotten

"Our defense system is insufficient," declared Mr. Sato in 1968. He abandoned all his reservations and launched an important press campaign to condition the Japanese public to the necessity of developing autonomous means of defense. The writer Ishihara, the playboy of Japanese politics and an open advocate of rearmament, was elected to advise the Lower House, uniting behind him 3 million voices. The Minister of Finance, Fukuda, did not hesitate to suggest that the pacifist constitution "imposed by the American occupants" should be completely revised. At the end of 1970, Mr. Sato chose as Minister of Defense Mr. Nakasone, young Turk of the Conservative party, whose ideas on this subject are arresting: Japan, he thinks, should free itself from military dependence on the United States and must be prepared not only to protect herself all alone, but to retaliate against any aggressive act against her. He would favor the development of a powerful military industrial machine.

A few years ago, such a position would have provoked a national outcry. But "national defense," an excellent euphemism for rearmament, is no longer a taboo subject.

The Japanese people are no longer ashamed to reveal their nationalism and are prepared to protect the prosperity they are so proud of. The reversal of public opinion on rearmament was lightning swift. Five out of six Japanese now support the army they had previously denounced; one able-bodied man out of two declares himself ready to volunteer to defend the mother country if she were "provoked" by a foreign power; the uniform is no longer looked at contemptuously; for a girl to marry a soldier is no longer the height of ignominy. While the older officers at the Yokosuka military academy consider the army a career, most of the young cadets told me that they enlisted out of patriotic idealism and felt they had a national mission to fulfil. No one listens to the leftists who still favor disarmament and neutralism in the belief that in case of attack Japan could count on the U.N. to defend her. The armaments makers have been given the green light and are no longer ashamed to announce the acceleration of their industry.

Even the famous "nuclear allergy" of the Japanese is being cured. Hiroshima and Nagasaki are almost forgotten, along with their 250,000 dead. The few dozens of victims who fall prey to radio-activity each year are in carefully guarded hospitals; they are symbols of the national humiliation, and society does nothing to help rehabilitate them by finding them jobs. They are the forgotten men.

Paradoxically, it is the foreigners who keep alive the memory of the bomb and who heap condolences on the Japanese. Many Western journalists still think they should begin every article they write about Japan with a reference to the Hiroshima holocaust. Critics of the United States seize every occasion to throw the atom bomb up to Americans.

I beg the reader's indulgence for a slight digression, unconstrained by moral considerations. In the minds of some people, the hideous events at Hiroshima and Nagasaki have martyrized Japan and have thus exculpated her of the crime of war, of the bloody reign of terror she imposed on those she conquered, and of the millions of deaths for which she alone was responsible.

Let us face the facts squarely. The Japanese were prepared to fight to the end. The United States had warned Japan about the terrifying weapon she had ready to use. Japanese representatives were invited to attend an atomic explosion. They refused. The bombs of Hiroshima and of Nagasaki made it possible to avoid an even more frightful blood bath of which Okinawa was an alarming foretaste. If the war had continued, hundreds of thousands, possibly even millions more would have gone to their tragic deaths. The bombs stopped the invasion of Japan by Soviet soldiers, which if it had taken place, might have resulted in a divided Japan, much like Korea and Germany. The atom bomb could actually be regarded as a "baptism of peace," however dramatic. It certainly made Japan one of the most pacifist nations in the world for twenty-five years.

Should Japan Be Prepared
with an Atomic Bomb?

In 1960, 5 percent of the Japanese interviewed answered yes. In 1965, the number had risen to 20 percent; in 1970, to 50 percent.

Japan as a nuclear power is a subject that no longer makes the crowds take to the streets; it is constantly discussed in business and government and social circles. Newspaper editorials are no longer afraid to address the issue.

In the Defense Ministry it is no longer forbidden to talk about the atomic bomb or about the carriers that would be needed to transport it. Ken Okuba, president of the Association of Industries for National Defense, advocates the stockpiling of nuclear arms. Former Prime Minister Kishi openly affirms: "Japan must have an atom bomb." His brother, the present prime minister, despite his virtuous public promises, whispers to Japanese executives: "It is regrettable that in this modern era we do not possess an atomic weapon."

Should a crisis come, 100 million patriots will undoubtedly give their unanimous support to the development of a complete nuclear arsenal.

According to Japanese specialists, it would not take more than a year or two at the most for Japanese scientists to put together an atomic bomb. They have already demonstrated that they know how to produce plutonium. If the United States were to cut off their important supplies of uranium, Japan could still buy it in Canada or in other countries where she is prepared to exploit it herself (like in Nigeria, in cooperation with France); or she could simply extract it from her own ground. It is thought that Japanese scientists don't have access to experimental proving grounds, but the sparsely inhabited Bonin islands could serve very well for this purpose. As for a carrier, there is the American Phantom produced under contract in Japan. Besides, in about five or six years Japan will probably have its own rockets of medium reach. Japan manufactures submarines and will be ready to launch nuclear cargo under water.

Today, Japan has a "self-defense" force of 265,000 volunteers: 180,000 infantrymen, 45,000 airmen, and 40,000 seamen. Reserves and national guard, if called up, would bring the figure to 325,000. As in most professional armies, there are too many officers in the Japanese forces. But this surplus will facilitate expansion of the Japanese Army. Military equipment is far from negligible.*

An astounding fact is that today, Japan manufactures or assembles under American contract practically all her armaments. She even sells a good bit to the Americans for Vietnam. But her manufactures are shipped to South Korea, and there stamped "Made in Korea"—just in case anybody should ask.

Japan's military expenditures are less than 1 percent of her gross national product, the lowest rate in the world.

*Ground: 720 tanks, 570 armored vehicles, 350 helicopters, 5,000 pieces of artillery, 600 ground-air Hawk rockets and 300 Nike Hercules rockets, 72 Nike Ajax batteries.
Air: 1,000 planes, including 200 F-104's and 35 Phantoms.
Sea: 550 vessels, including about 50 destroyers, 13 submarines, 250 aero-naval aircraft.

The U.S. spends 66 times as much, or 10 percent of its gross national product; China and the U.S.S.R. also spend 10 percent, and France spends 5.5 percent. But, as has been said, the government now envisages a military complex as powerful as the industrial complex. The defense budget was doubled for 1972.

By 1976, Japan should have the third largest navy in the world, right up there after the U. S. and Russia, and ahead of China.

For air defense, Japan has chosen the American Phantom jet. She will be manufacturing over a hundred of these under contract. It goes without saying that Japan has excellent pilots to handle these aircraft.

An electronic anti-aircraft system has already been blueprinted. Mitsubishi is hounding the government for a contract to manufacture purely Japanese fighter-bombers. So are Nissan and Fuji, who provided Japan with 25,000 aircraft, including the famous Zeroes during World War II.

By 1976, Japan will be the most powerful of the non-nuclear countries. Her military budget will equal that of Great Britain and of France. Within the next 20 years, she will forge ahead of France, Great Britain, and Germany, put together. Yet for many Japanese military and business leaders, this rate of development is insufficient.

One cannot help ask the question: What danger does a rearmed Japan represent?

Dangerous Despite Herself

Japan has very unpleasant memories of war. She has no aggressive designs. She has no enemies, and no one threatens her. So what purpose would a powerful army serve? Mr. Sato replies:

> . . . *to protect our prosperity and assume our growing international obligations, particularly in relation to the stability of Asia.*

A policy of neutrality, in the style of the Swiss or Swedes, is not possible for Japan because of her geographic position at the feet of the two Communist giants, and because of her alliance with America, but chiefly because of her economic and political ambitions.

Japan wants to insure her defense, yes. But the problem is where to draw the lines. At her coastline? No. Tokyo set the limits in 1970: The line of defense crosses the Korean peninsula, passes through the Straits of Formosa, then stops on the dotted line . . . (does it continue invisibly until the Straits of Malacca?) In any case, the security of the island of Taiwan is deemed "important" for the security of Japan, and the security of South Korea is considered "essential."

Conclusion: If the soldiers of North Korea cross or

threaten to cross the demilitarized zone set in 1953—there are small incidents of this sort every day—Japan may react. A member of the Japanese government announced in Parliament that he would not consider it unconstitutional to send military advisers, and even troops, to South Korea for "peaceful tasks" if Seoul so requested. The parallel to the U.S. escalation in Vietnam is obvious.

Japan wants military power in order to protect her prosperity. But what does this imply? "Mistress of the high seas and of international straits," says the minister of defense about the security of the supply routes. The fleet sails farther and farther away around the coast of the archipelago. The official visit of a Japanese squadron to Singapore in October, 1969, did not go unnoticed.

The government considers that, in a crisis, the dispatch of a warship to a foreign port "would not violate the pacifist Constitution of Japan on condition that the seamen do not debark." But perhaps tomorrow the government will decide: The seamen can go down to the wharf on condition that they do not go away from it. And so on. What would Japan's reaction be if the Straits of Malacca, through which passes 90 percent of the petroleum she imports from the Near East, were to be blocked one day?

The protection of Japan's prosperity can go very far. To guarantee the safety of Japan's foreign investments in Southeast Asia, for example, requires stable political regimes in these countries. First, economic aid is furnished. Then arms, to maintain order. Then "specialists" are sent; then "advisers". . . The sequence is familiar.

What do Japan's neighbors say? The only countries rejoicing in Japan's military power and ambitions are South Korea and Formosa, whose protector Japan has become. Japan's old enemies watch her anxiously. In Jakarta and Manila fear is openly expressed and some people talk about the renaissance of Japanese militarism. This certainly is the point of view of Peking and of Pyongyang, both of whom accuse Japan of wanting to become the "policeman of Asia." The sudden reconciliation between China and North Korea (whose relations were chilled during the Chinese cultural revolution) the day after the Sato-Nixon agreement is significant. Even in the United States and in Australia voices are raised to denounce the potential menace of a rearmed Japan.

Distinguished observers have remarked that there is no reason why Japan would enter into conflict with another country or why she should embark on another military venture. It is difficult to fault them without having recourse to seemingly extravagant hypotheses. But when one has observed the Japanese economy functioning like a well-organized army; when one considers the Japanese disposition toward military discipline, their taste for order and respect for authority; when one is aware that certain big companies require their young recruits to serve a period of three-weeks training in the army in order "to harden them and sharpen their patriotism"; when one knows that in certain political and business circles a compulsory draft is wholeheartedly endorsed; when one has seen uniforms constantly and happily worn by schoolchildren and by workmen, making the streets look as though the country were already in a state of general mobilization; when one imagines what might happen if the Soka Gakkai came into power, or if an economic crisis developed, or if Japan were menaced by a foreign power—one must feel apprehensive.

Kamikazis of the Revolution

Most of the student radicals in Japan are mildly communist, and favor reform without violence. The extremists are only a small minority. The student organization, the Zengakuren, claims 150,000 adherents, although the authorities place the count at 80,000, out of a total student population of 1,500,-000. The association is one of the best organized in the world. But, in Japan, three years of combat have produced nothing. Japan is decidedly less than ever a revolutionary country. Early in 1970, the universities were paralyzed or shut down, but higher education has not yet undergone the slightest reform. The military alliance with the United States was easily consummated. The government is stronger than ever.

Leftist students encountered police repression unequaled in the West. Student troops were decimated and their leaders were severely punished. In Spring, 1970, two or three thousand of them were in prisons, serving sentences ranging from a few months to two years. To take on small or large numbers of students who have become skilled at street fighting, special anti-riot police troops have been trained and mobilized.

The failure of the left wing in Japan is due mostly to the indifference of a very passive public opinion, which has been regimented by the economic organization, and seduced and preoccupied with materialistic gains made available by the society of abundance. Society is bored with the goings on of the young extremists. For a year or two the spectacular encounters between students and police were a source of diversion. But after the culmination of student activism in January, 1969, with the occupation of Yasuda Hall at Tokyo University, the leftists offered nothing more of interest.

For two days, 400 students held several million TV spectators spellbound. Hour by hour, they watched a spectacle which in our era can normally be seen only in the movies: the storming, in the purest medieval style, by 8,000 police of the last bastion of resistance on the Todaï campus. The elite of the leftist student shock troops were entrenched in Yasuda Hall, now transformed into a redoubtable fortress. Its portal of Gothic arches had been completely barricaded. Molotov cocktails and chemical bombs replaced the boiling oil of olden days. The steady stream of bazooka fire, grenades, and tear gas issuing from the student assailants reminded one of the catapults at the ancient scenes of bombardment.

The second day, the police action began in earnest. They demolished the barricades with electric saws and blowtorches, and, mounting ladders, inserted water pipes into the crevices of the walls. From the skies, helicopters dropped hundreds of quarts of liquid asphyxiants. The battle waged up to the staircase of the highest central turret. Yasuda finally fell after 48 hours of siege. Since that time, fed up with violence, people take no more interest in the "lunatics" of Zengakuren.

The student extremists have been denounced by every left-wing party. They were not successful in attracting the sympathy of the young workers whom they wooed. Divided into multiple factions and fighting constantly among themselves, motivated by doctrines and philosophies which are abstract and confused, they seem now to be completely spent. They wanted to disrupt the Osaka exposition, but they failed completely. The Tokyo chief of police was justified in saying they were nothing more than "soap bubbles."

These *enfants terribles* are no more than a weak minority. The majority of students adjust to the world they live in and ask few questions. The golden youth of the night clubs, sports cars, fashion boutiques want the good life. The leftists are isolated. Most of them know that sooner or later they will be absorbed into the society they now oppose, and that they will end up by serving big business, along with their elders, who fought in radical movements in the sixties and caused the downfall of Kishi. They take advantage of their youth in order to taste a freedom that has no place in the adult world.

The real extremists are fanatical. These kamikazes of violence have formed a "red army" which acts with the force of despair. These "desperadoes" were responsible for the hijacking of a Tokyo-Seoul JAL Boeing in March, 1970. They have bombed police stations and even the residence of the prime minister. They commandeered a ferryboat. They are relentlessly pursued by the police who have followed them right to their training retreats hidden in the mountains. Half of the troops of the red army are in prison. A few hundred are still at large. But Japan has not heard the last of them yet.

Learning to Think

Toward the end of 1967, the Zengakuren sparked a revolt against Japan's ancient university system. They protested against Japanese professors who were benumbed with a sense of their own prestige, dogmatic in their beliefs, and authoritarian in attitude. They protested against a university admissions system which excluded so many students because there was no room in the free universities and private universities, while less selective, were too costly. Japanese university students are not as affluent as Western students; most of them have to work part-time and during their vacations to support themselves through college. Private universities receive very little aid from the government. To survive they have to accept any student who can afford their fees; as a consequence their diplomas have very little value. The level of instruction is much inferior to the standards that prevail in private universities in the West.

Only those privileged to attend state universities can look forward to favorable careers. The Zengakuren oppose prevailing conditions which doom children, from the earliest ages, to be brutalized in order to climb aboard the elevator that leads to big business. Before one can embark on the pathway to success, one must pass rigorous college entrance exams. These exams have been responsible for quite a number of student suicides. The bachelor's degree is a must; failure is regarded as a family and social tragedy. The exams actually test memory and not intelligence. Students are incensed to see the university become simply the workshop for prefabricated minds, made to serve industry. They reject a university and a society that preaches that you must think but does not teach you how to think.

The student rebellion has gone beyond the university; it has become politicized. The rebels now aim their shafts at the government. They abhor Japan's alliance with what they deem American imperialism. They oppose Japan's rearmament program and her nationalistic ambitions. They inveigh against the capitalists who seduce and robotize their employees with paternalistic appeasements. The final thing that the Zengakuren reject the public can neither understand nor accept because it is so sacrosanct to the Japanese: They do not "buy" progress and more progress, and still more progress spurred on by the relentless hammer of automation. The new Japanese society for them spells total alienation, and opposing this has become their battle cry.

What, after all, is the promise of this new society? Material security for which the people pay in dehumanization; well-organized "happiness" in exchange for the abnegation of individualism.

Concrete and Wax Paper

Japanese cities are notoriously ugly. Even the most venerated symbols of the past are not spared the ugliest manifestations of progress. A cement factory might be installed directly opposite a temple; a blast furnace might rise next to a beautiful shrine; a road might be cut through an ancient park.

Concrete is devouring the sanctuaries; it is brought in to save the worm-eaten wood. A horrible concrete platform was erected around the excellent Kamakura Buddha.

At Nara, a vulgar, gaudy Dreamland, copied from the Californian Disneyland, has defiled the cradle of Japanese civilization. The silence of the moss gardens is shattered by thunderous loudspeakers.

A monstrous tower, which only foreigners tried in vain to prevent, mars the ancient imperial capital of Japan: Kyoto no longer is the Florence of the Orient. Imagine a permanent carnival of prizes, hot dogs, and souvenirs in the park of Versailles; imagine concrete cubes surrounding Notre Dame Cathedral; imagine jukebox music in the Statue of Liberty. Add to this image all the papers and debris left by picknickers.

The Japanese who maintain they are nature lovers are among the worst pollutors of the world. Without batting an eye, they allow industries to build factories on their beaches, and to transform the sea into a sewage hole of industrial waste. They seem not to notice the despoiling of the most charming countrysides by a profusion of electric wiring and signposts.

Not one voice is raised to protest this constant rape of the most sacred treasures of the past, this ruination of pastoral landscapes and majestic mountainsides. No rule, no law opposes it. The tourist, no matter how dirty, how disrespectful, how noisy, is king. Neither beauty, nor poetry, nor history can change the course of this frenetic race toward modernization.

Inspiration in Exile

Japan's culture is flagging. To paraphrase Paul Valéry: Too much technique leaves too little soul. Intellectual asphyxiation has deadened the creative imagination of Japan's artists and writers. Authentic Japanese artists who wish to express themselves freely must choose between being ignored in their own country or exiling themselves to another. Those who wish to survive at home must imitate the West or sacrifice their talents to the press or to the large stores and businesses that are the temples of modern Japan. For the last 15 years, sculpture and painting has stagnated. What is being produced now is, with rare exception, derivative.

The symbol of this lethargy in Tokyo, where public works of art are scarce, is the Ginza clock, by Taro Okamoto, a sad copy in three dimensions of a Miro. The plastic arts, functional art, and architecture do show creative imagination.

Actually the cultural life, although uninspired, is very active in Tokyo. Exhibits of every kind are constantly organized by the public relations departments of the big department stores. Concerts by the great artists of the world are plentiful; but the concert halls of Tokyo will only accept artists with known names. The Japanese artist must make his reputation abroad before he is invited to perform at home.

The delightful *Bunraku* (puppet theater) performs only several times a year and its audience has been very sparse. But on its return to the Japanese capital after a triumphant tour of Europe in 1968, crowds appeared to applaud the performances that the Occidentals had received so enthusiastically. The mysterious smile on the white mask of the *Noh* performer seems to freeze in pathetic astonishment before the half-empty house.

Happily, the dull and stereotyped Western-style theater is being challenged by a burgeoning of young, avant-garde acting groups, performing in coffee shops and basements. The modern works they perform, written by young authors, are uneven in quality, but at least they evidence an attempt to be experimental and imaginative.

As for movies, Kurosawa, the director of *The Seven Samurai* and *Rashomon*, a Cannes Festival winner in 1951, has left for Hollywood. Kobayashi and Ichikawa no longer make films. The withdrawal of these three cinematic giants of the golden age of Japan's seventh art tells a great deal about the deplorable state of Japan's film industry today. The cinematic crisis precipitated by TV has resulted in the closing of many movie houses because of severely reduced attendance. The five big studios who control the production and distribution of most of the films have turned, for the most part, to erotico-productions. They also produce some science fiction as their genre grows in popularity; and occasionally they produce an historical epic. Love stories or light romantic comedies are hopelessly inane.

A few talented independent directors—Oshima (*The Hanging*), Mamura (*The Man Without a Map*), Teshighara (*The Woman in the Dunes*), and Kumäi and Shindo—are working on some very interesting films. They may be the hope of the future.

As for literature, there are few signs of vitality. Dazai,

the last humanist of Japanese literature, committed suicide in 1948. Kawabata, the Nobel Prize laureate of 1968, is the last name in a great literary tradition. Mishima, the most brilliant writer of his generation, sought to fill the spiritual void by turning to the past. He, too, killed himself. The former president of the Japanese Pen Club, Serizawa, sums up the situation thus:

> *The young people are now writing only for magazines, which stifles their creative energy and curtails their inventiveness. They drown themselves in popular, commercial literature. We have too many books, but not enough serious writers. The novice writer's plight is similar to the fate of fruit: to fill the demand they were made to grow too fast, and lost their flavor.*

A professor of letters of Todaï explained to me:

> *Japanese literature is almost wholly derivative. There was the existentialist vogue, then the new novel, now it's structuralism. The big shame is that most professors of literature are not interested in Japanese literature at all, but only in foreign literature.*

Slavish imitation of the West has stifled the artistic creation and the cultural life of the country. Before the war, two civilizations managed to coexist and survive. The defeat and subjugation of Japan traumatized her to the point where she felt she had to discard the system of values which led her to disaster. On this spiritually devastated terrain has risen the cult of the golden calf. One constantly hears that traditions are balls and chains which must be abolished. Indifference to their cultural heritage has turned into contempt for most young people who are fiercely determined to resemble Westerners. The *Noh* theater and the tea ceremony are meaningless to them. They put chairs on their tatamis. Official propaganda pretends to be effecting a synthesis between East and West. But the fact is that Japan is no longer truly Eastern, nor is she truly Western. Japan has become an anomaly adrift in the Far East.

To reassure themselves of some kind of identity, the Japanese still boast of their traditions, now no more solid than a cream puff. The consumer society has recently revived for its leisure life some of the traditional costumes and folklore: kimonos worn in the evenings in their own homes, the honorable bath, the cherry blossoms, and the appreciation of the beauty of the four seasons. Mishima has said that the Japanese confuse "conduct" with "culture." The customs and costumes that are unique to Japan could prove that she has not renounced her past and will one day again have a vibrant culture. Of traditional Japan there remains only the formalism and a few mental reflexes. This country appears to have lost its soul. The identity crisis, with which intellectuals and artists are preoccupied, pervades their best work. Their work is characterized by a total absence of gaiety; instead there is always the ominous atmosphere of a sinister, brutal world.

In the avant-garde theater of happenings, where spectators sit right next to the actors and are invited to participate in the drama, the young comedians seem to be propelled by the implacable law of the machine and by the force of social pressure; their presumably absurd mumblings are nothing more than pleas for a return to the lost values of love, freedom, and, above all, respect for individuality.

The lack of imagination was epitomized in Taro Okamoto's sun tower at the Osaka exposition. This altogether puerile and ugly work which passed for humor didn't even have the charm or forcefulness of being deliberately absurd.

Mao knew that to preserve the revolutionary spirit of China he had to say no to the machine. Viewed from the vantage point of modernized Japan, there is something refreshing about Mao's cultural revolution.

Twenty-Five Cents for a Jar of Fresh Air

Japanese cities are inhuman. Except perhaps for Tokyo and Kyoto, trees and green spaces are rare or nonexistent. The state and the local communities have neglected their duty to the people in favor of industry.

Many cities have no drainage systems; two thirds of Tokyo itself is deprived of adequate sewage removal. Industries, highways, and railways are built wherever it is deemed profitable, scandalously ignoring the public welfare. Because of noise hospitals, nurseries, and schools are forced to move out. The pollution level in Japan has reached frightful proportions unequaled anywhere else. From Tokyo, the profile of Fuji rising in the horizon was a familiar sight. These days, you can only see Fuji when there is a high wind.

A study showed that on days when pollution reaches the dangerous stage, the number of deaths rises appreciably. Water and air pollution in and around Tokyo and other cities has already killed hundreds of people; hundreds of others are hospitalized suffering from respiratory sicknesses or from having ingested fish from contaminated rivers. The companies responsible for these deaths and illnesses pay negligible fines when a court has found them guilty.

Certain neighborhoods surrounding particular industrial complexes have disappeared entirely. In Kawasaki, near Tokyo, where furnaces and chimneys burn and spew 24 hours a day, infants commonly suffer from asthma and schoolchildren wear surgical masks going to and from school. These masks, usually worn by Japanese to avoid colds, are more and more being used to filter the polluted air that threatens their health.

In Tokyo, in the streets and parks, the trees twist their defoliated skeletal branches toward the deadly fumes, and die. Many of the cherry trees no longer blossom. In the countryside around these cities, certain species of insects are disappearing, notably the butterfly. In the Sumida River, which crosses Tokyo, there is no longer a single fish; on its murky banks, rats and water spiders run rampant.

In the streets, in the stations and stores you see people gulping down bottles of vitamin-enriched juice. This is as popular in Japan as Coca-Cola is in the United States. It is the elixir of long life. Vending machines sell jars of fresh air for twenty-five cents.

"Shigatakanai," say the Japanese, and they shrug their shoulders. "There's nothing we can do." This is the price of progress. The lambs go to slaughter without protest.

Life in a Sardine Can

Fifty million Japanese live crowded together in an area of 3,000 square miles—the greatest density in the world. In 1985 there will be 75 million living in the same area.

On Sundays and holidays, this enormous mass of people heads for the countryside. On the highways, the traffic jams are incredible. The lakes, rivers, beaches, mountain retreats are all built up. On certain Sundays the lines to climb Fuji are backed up for miles. In one weekend, 2,500,000 people invade a small stretch of beaches from Ayiama to Enoshima. On Sunday evenings these beaches all smell of urine.

For the opening of the shellfish season in Chiba near Tokyo, over 100,000 people flock to one beach in one day. For a fee of twenty-five cents each person gets a few square feet of sand to explore. By nightfall not a single clam is left. In a park at Osaka, two people were trampled to death by the crowds disgorged by hundreds of buses to see the cherry blossoms in bloom.

But the Japanese do not mind. The herding, the long queues, traffic jams, all this never puts them in a bad mood. They feel safe in this kind of "togetherness."

In Japan, Aldous Huxley's prophetic *Brave New World* seems about to become a reality. The signs of this are everywhere.

In a vineyard near Tokyo you can harvest the grapes for $3.00 an hour to the tune of French music played over loudspeakers. On their terraces, some of the large department stores offer their clients a bit of the disappearing country. Children gambol in a miniature, fenced-in forest. They can catch butterflies and other insects which their mothers have paid for.

Entire species of insects which the stores have carried off especially for the nature-loving children are in danger of extinction.

On the roofs of buildings, any free space, however small, is fenced in and used for sports activities; tennis is played against a wall, baseballs are attached to a string, golf is practiced in cages.

The loudspeakers which infest the country are without doubt the most odious scourge of modern Japan. One cannot escape their implacable tyranny. In the streets and stores, they blare their interminable promotions. They howl in forests and on the beaches and mountains. Even ski slopes are awakened at 6 A.M. with their piercing reveille. On public transport the names of the stations are untiringly recited. I once asked a Japanese who had visited France for the first time what had impressed him the most in Paris. After a moment of reflection he said: "They do not announce the stops in the buses or subways."

The Japanese are already living in the synthetic era. Indifferent to the quality of natural fabric, they almost always dress in synthetic materials. In their homes, plastic replaces wood, metal, and leather; it has even begun to replace the straw of the venerable tatami. Plastic renders flower arrangements (*ikebanas*) eternal. The production of plastic, synthetics, and cardboard per person is higher in Japan than it is in all the Common Market countries. And of course neon is king. Not even bed lamps are spared. The ordinary classic light bulb is rare and acquires an infinite charm in Japan. In the park at Nara, there are stuffed does to make picture-taking simpler for the camera fiends.

The chemically grown vegetables and fruits sprout up quickly thanks to huge doses of chemicals, and have very little taste. Bread is sold in artificial colors—pink, green, purple. Scientists have just produced a synthetic meat created from petroleum by-products.

"Progress and Harmony for Humanity" was the theme of the Osaka exposition. One could see a great deal of technical progress, but not much harmony. What did Japan really exhibit? Is this progress the work of humans, or of robots? Gadgetry is plentiful, but where is peace of spirit? Is there not more noise than music? We are closed in by walls of plaster, plastic, and rubber without windows to look out of. Beauty and poetry are anachronisms, part of a forgotten, congealed past. Japan is a puerile world of science fiction, a humorless farce, a celebration without joy. Japan is a vision of the future—bleak and sinister, depressing and infinitely frightening.

Index

Index